WHAT'S BLOCKING YOUR CONFIDENCE

EFFECTIVE WAYS TO CONQUER YOUR FEARS

SECOND EDITION

LASHANA LLOYD

WHAT'S BLOCKING YOUR CONFIDENCE?

Effective Ways to Conquer Your Fears
Second Edition

LASHANA LLOYD

WHAT'S BLOCKING YOUR CONFIDENCE?

Effective Ways to Conquer Your Fears

Second Edition

Faith Led Life, LLC

401 East Jackson Street

Suite 2340

Tampa, FL 33602

www.faithledlife.com

ISBN: 979-8-218-01714-9

Printed in the United States of America

Library of Congress Control Number: 2022919424

DEDICATION

To God, my Father, thank You for creating me in Your image, breathing life into me, and allowing me to be here to carry out this assignment for the glory of Your Kingdom You call me Your daughter every day, and I take great honor in that. You knew me inside and out, flaws and all, yet You still wanted to use me to draw Your creation back to Your heart. Thank you for believing in me, encouraging me, and having faith in me. Even during the times when I wanted to give up on myself (and even tried to give up on myself), You refused to let that happen. You are always able to see greater in me than I will ever know.

To Jesus Christ, my Best Friend, thank You for breaking through the stony layers of my heart and showing me what true love really is. You, being innocent, knew that I was guilty, but You took the fall for my sins by allowing Yourself to be a sacrifice so that Your blood could cleanse me of my sins. You showed me the way to take and I have been following You ever since. Continue to allow Your love to flow through me as I continue to receive the love that You have for me.

To the Holy Spirit, my Comforter, thank You for living inside of me and living through me. You lead and guide me every moment of every day of my life, and You never lead me wrong. I lovingly commend You for ordering my steps and never leaving me alone on this earth. I'm grateful for how You speak to me and how You live through me.

CONTENTS

TESTIMONIALS

"This message is as informative as it is profound! It is a great reminder that fear does not come from God but it comes in the form of a spirit from the enemy named Satan. It also reminds us that there is a difference between the healthy fear that we should have towards God and the unhealthy fear than can create bondage if left unchecked.

I can attest to this type of paralytic fear that is described in this message. I have allowed this type of unhealthy fear to paralyze me for many years. Although I still struggle with it, the reverence I have for God, which is defined as healthy fear, is consuming me more and more every day. It is a spiritual battle! This message gives us tools on how to fight and win."

— YANICK KANE, CHILDREN'S AUTHOR
WWW.YANICKKANE.COM

"Resist Taking the Bait was a very eye-opening chapter for me. I love that she gives a practical exercise for conquering your fears, a tangible method you can use and implement to face your fears head-on. I will definitely put this practice into action and ask God to give me the strength to push forward. It's time to break the chains of fear in Jesus' Name!"

— FELICIA JOHNSON, FEDERAL
GOVERNMENT EMPLOYEE

"False Evidence Appearing Real (F.E.A.R.) is a lie we all face, and it is one of the fiery darts the enemy uses to deter us from our God-appointed destiny. However, "Whom the son sets free is truly free indeed." In her book, What's Blocking Your Confidence? LaShana exposes the enemy of our souls and the lie called "fear" that he uses against us to distract, deter or abort our destinies. LaShana shares her personal journey from being bound by fear to being transformed into freedom through Christ Jesus. She shares Scripture, insight, and practical guidelines for defeating fear. What's Blocking Your Confidence? was timely and has impacted my life. It will be a tool that I will reference and share with my clients who wrestle with the spirit of fear. Second Timothy 1:7 resonates throughout this book: "For God did not give us a spirit of fear but of power and of love and of a sound mind." Thank you, LaShana, for your obedience in writing and sharing this book with the world. God's continued and richest Blessings!!!"

~

INTRODUCTION

There are so many people in the world today who are living lives God didn't create them to live. They are living beneath a standard that doesn't grant the Father's approval. They want more for themselves; they know they should have more, but there's one thing in particular that is stopping them from going beyond the boundaries of that they wish to have - they are living in fear.

Fear has stopped so many people from moving forward. It is the reason why some people feel stuck and are not able to move forward. For others, they have lived in fear for so long, they feel comfortable remaining in that state. How can this be? Why is it important to do something about this? Is there anything that can be done to change this? The answer is a resounding YES!

This book was written for you if you are ready to move past your fears and walk in your God-given confidence. This book is for you if you are tired of circling this mountain, and you are ready to live a life that is free of fear as well other components (which are discussed in this book) that are attached to fear. Or maybe you are tired of not being able to progress because of fear, but you are not sure what steps you have to take to move on. Regardless of your background, social status, or position, if you are ready to be set free, this is a must-read book!

This book was NOT written for you if you choose to remain stuck in your way of thinking and you do not want to change your negative thinking about fear. This is not a book I recommend you read if you choose to accept fear and refuse to fight for the confidence that God has given to you that was stolen from you by the enemy (Satan). It's not a book for you to read if you refuse to believe what God has said about your confidence and spoken against your fears. I dare not waste your time if want to remain spiritually imprisoned and refuse to be set free from an invisible state that has been holding you hostage and blocking your confidence.

You do not have to stay where you are by walking in fear. Your confidence awaits you on the other side of fear. Trust in God and believe that He has greater in store for you that doesn't involve you being fearful and unable to live the best life you could ever live. Believe what Apostle Paul said in 2 Timothy 1:7 because it's true: *"for God has not given us a spirit of fear, but of power, and of love, and of a sound mind"* (LSV). The Father didn't create you to live in fear; He created you for His glory and to live out your purpose for Him.

I know from firsthand experience what it feels like to live in fear. When I chose to live in fear, I chose to forfeit the right to live out a life that was satisfying and pleasing to the Father. I was this shy, closed-in, and isolated person who was satisfied with living that way. I gave the spirit of fear a chair to sit in and take up residency in my life, and I had no problem with doing that. Fear became my crutch. It became my twisted safe haven and my validation for so many excuses that I made for it. But all of that changed over time as I moved further into my Christian walk and tapped into who God says I am (through His Word and through speaking to me) and how it is impossible to walk in fear and confidence at the same time.

I wrote this book because I want to help you break free from fear so that you can walk in the confidence that God has for you. As you walk in confidence, you will see the peace, contentment, and sense of freedom that it will bring you. No more will the enemy be able to keep you suppressed and hold you in bondage because as Jesus said in John 8:36 (WEB), *"If therefore the Son makes you free, you will be free indeed."* My prayer is that you will take the tools that are written in this book and apply them to your daily life. I pray that you will embrace the confidence that God has given to you so that you can embrace the life that God has for you. May you no longer feel the need to hide in fear but choose to stand in the confidence that is available to you. As you trust in the Father more, you will be able to trust in plans that He has for you so that you live confidently and freely in Him. In Jesus' Name I pray, Amen.

Walk in your confidence,

LaShana Lloyd

1

FACING YOUR FEARS HEAD-ON

What is Fear?

In order to understand how to face your fears head-on, you must first know what fear is. According to Merriam-Webster's Dictionary, fear is "*an unpleasant, often strong emotion caused by anticipation or awareness of danger (an instance of this emotion or a state marked by this emotion). It is a form of being anxious and concerned (solicitude)* [1] *When viewed from a medical perspective, fear is the unpleasant emotional state consisting of psychological and psychophysiological responses to a real external threat or danger. Fear is also the response to a real or imagined perception of danger. An inappropriate or abnormal level of fear is called a phobia.*" [2]

From a Biblical standpoint, fear is profound reverence and awe - especially towards God. Fear is also a reason for alarm due to danger. The Biblical definition of fear can be explained in two ways. First, there is the positive side of fear. Proverbs 9:10 (NIV) says, "*The fear of the Lord is the beginning of wisdom."* When you fear God in this manner, you are showing that you respect Him because of the power and authority He has. This is the type of fear the Father wants us to have towards Him.

However, there is a difference between fearing God and being fearful of God. When you serve God out of fear of who He is, you are able to operate out of relationship and fellowship towards Him. On the other hand, when you serve God because you are fearful of Him, are operating out of bondage. What I mean by this is you see God as One who sits back and waits for you to mess up so that He can condemn you to hell. So, because you are fearful, you try to do everything by "your" book because of this picture you have painted in your mind about Him. In reality, the Father loves us, and it is His strong desire that we seek Him for being the loving God that He is. He does not want you to spend the rest of your life walking on eggshells and becoming self-righteous; He wants you to seek Him for the righteousness He has for you to receive through His Son, Jesus Christ.

Where Does Fear Come From?

"For God hath not given us the spirit of fear; but of power, and of love, and of a sound mind."

— 2 TIMOTHY 1:7 (KJV)

According to 2 Timothy 1:7, fear is a spirit that does not come from God; it is a spirit that is sent by the enemy. The enemy knows that if he can succeed with getting the spirit of fear to operate in our lives, he will be able to destroy us from the inside out. Fear can come in many forms and operate in many ways. Fear can rob you of your joy. It can cause you to become bound by negative thoughts and negative actions, and it causes you to remain stuck in the past. Most importantly, if the enemy can carry this out successfully, the spirit of fear could stop you from living out your purpose and walking in your destiny. To some, this may not be a big deal, but when it comes to the enemy, if he can stop you from walking in your God-given purpose and moving towards your destiny, he can stop you from destroying him. This is why it is important to know who you are and where you stand in this spiritual battle. So, I ask you, where does fear come from?

Our Own Imagination

Your mind is constantly at work; that's why it is important in *"casting down imaginations, and every high thing that exalteth itself against the knowledge of God, and bringing into captivity every thought to the obedience of Christ"* (2 Corinthians 10:5, KJV). This is why it is imperative to bind and rebuke ungodly thoughts (especially thoughts pertaining to fear), get into God's Word, and pray so that the enemy will not be able to plant any seeds in your mind and hold you hostage with fear.

Traumatic Experiences

In 2011, while I was serving in the Army, I was deployed for six months. Throughout this deployment, the forward operating base I was assigned to came under attack often. This would involve rounds being fired at our base as an attempt to destroy our vehicles, our facilities, and our lives. There were plenty of mornings when I would be awakened out of my sleep by the rounds the enemies in that area would launch at our base. Whenever this would happen, everybody in our living quarters would have to get up, quickly put on our protective gear, go outside, head to the nearest bunker, and stay there until we received notification that it was safe for us to go back to our living quarters. This happened on numerous occasions while I was on this deployment. The noise these rounds made was so distinctive and so piercing that even after I redeployed, I could still remember the whistling sounds they would make coming toward our base followed by the loud boom after they struck something.

For a while after I redeployed, I suffered from post-traumatic stress disorder (PTSD). I would get flashbacks and/or anxiety from an incident that would be initiated as a result of a traumatic event that happened in my life. For the longest time after I redeployed, I was terribly afraid of fireworks. New Year's Day and the Fourth of July were the worst holidays for me. I had no desire to buy fireworks or watch fireworks shows because the noise sounded similar to what I used to hear when rounds would be launched at our base.

A few years ago, I remember bringing in the New Year while celebrating in church. After the service was over, my whole demeanor changed. I could hear nothing but fireworks going off outside. It terrified me. To make matters worse, some church members ran to their vehicles and pulled out their boxes of fireworks so they could join in on the silent torture that I was enduring. I made a dash out of the church and tried to get to my car as quickly as I could, but it didn't help. As I was walking to my car, it seemed as if everybody who was in arms-length was shooting fireworks; it was irritating!

My heart started racing, my head was pounding, and I was breathing hard. Just moments earlier, I was worshipping and praising God but now, all I wanted to do was just make it to my car so that I could go home and lock myself in my room. Driving home was a bigger challenge than walking to my car. There were people all over the place shooting fireworks in the street, on the sidewalks, on the bridge, and on their front lawns. There was nowhere I could go to have even a second of silence. I was speeding, trying to get home. I was shaking, and clenching my steering wheel as tightly as I could. When I finally did make it home, I ran upstairs, slammed my door, put my earplugs in, jumped in my bed, and pulled the covers over my head. The way I was acting was brought on by what I went through on my deployment, but the overall cause as to why I continued to act like that was because of fear. Physically, I was no longer deployed; but psychologically, my mind was back in a place that I had left a while ago.

After going through this for some time, I cried out to God. I told Him, "Father, I need Your help; I really need Your help. I need my peace back. Please give me Your peace; just fill me with Your peace." The more I prayed this prayer, the less anxious, angry, and irritated I would get. Over time, I no longer found myself getting angry or anxious, but it took me wanting to be delivered from this fear in order for the deliverance to happen.

What Has You Walking in Fear?

Despite what you believe or how you may feel, you can face your fears head-on. There are several things that could have you walking in fear: generational curses, not renewing your mind, and walking by sight instead of faith.

Generational Curses

Generational curses are the sins (and consequences of sins) of ancestors that are passed down from one generation to the next. There are so many people - especially believers - who are bound by generational curses and some do not even realize it. This would explain why some people do the things they do, act the way they act, or feel the way they feel. This would be also the case with fear. The fear that someone has may be the result of fear that they witnessed in their parents who had witnessed from their parents and so on.

A minor example of this would be my mother and her fear of balloons. When I was growing up, I used to love playing with balloons that I had to stretch and blow the air into. When I would blow these balloons up around my mom, she would become terrified. She would tell me to get away from her or go into another room because she was afraid that the balloons would pop. One day, I was at a gathering and there were other children around me who were playing with balloons. I was not paying attention to one of them when all of a sudden, the balloon this child had popped so loud, it scared me. From that point on, I no longer wanted to play with or be around balloons anymore because of a fear that I learned from my mother.

A more severe example of a generational curse would be the abuse I witnessed and/or heard of happening with some of the women in my family - the main person being my mother. From the ages of three to twelve, I saw my father physically, verbally, and emotionally abuse my mother often. I also saw other women on both sides of my family who were abused in the same, similar, or worse manner. Seeing this as a child, I knew that it wasn't normal but wasn't sure what "normal" was. I saw what my mother went through and the pain she endured at the hands of my father; once, he almost killed her right in front of me. This, along with other things that I went through and witnessed, had hardened my heart to the point I would often tell myself, *I don't ever want to get married because I don't want to marry a man who comes off one way and then treats me the way Daddy treated Mama.* Seeing this go on in my house and hearing about and seeing it go on with other women in my family caused me to develop trust issues with men.

Not Renewing Your Mind

"Do not conform to the pattern of this world, but be transformed by the renewing of your mind. Then you will be able to test and approve what God's will is--his good, pleasing and perfect will."

— ROMANS 12:2 (NIV)

Our mind (our way of thinking) is much more powerful than what we realize. When I was an unbeliever, my thought process was much different from what it is now as a believer. I commonly thought in a way that was contrary to the Father because at that particular time in my life, the Holy Spirit was not living inside of me. I responded in a worldly way instead of God's way because my mind was not renewed. Because of that, I headed down some destructive paths primarily because of ungodly ways of thinking.

I was raised in the church and as a young child, I loved going to church, hearing about God, and enjoyed knowing how much Jesus loved me. However, as I approached my teenage years, my way of thinking became distorted by the enemy. He confused my mind so badly about being a Christian that I would justify my reasons as to why I did not want to go back to church as well as why I questioned God. This was mainly due to what I allowed myself to see, hear, and believe about what other "Christians" were doing. There were times when I would see certain church members stand on the church grounds smoking cigarettes before and after the service was over. I would hear stories about certain individuals at my church or other churches who had affairs, and some of these affairs resulted in a child or children being born. What part of that was "holy"?

These are just a few things I caught wind of that was going on. The more I discovered, the more confused and angrier I would get. I allowed my mind to form thoughts that I should not have and before I knew it, I found myself judging other people and assuming what I thought my walk with God was going to be like because of what I saw other people doing. I would say to myself, "*So you mean to tell me that even though*

Sister So and So is acting like this in the church or Brother So and So is doing this outside of the church, or with all the stuff that these groups of people are doing in another church is OK? They will still get to go to heaven doing/saying all the stuff that they are doing/saying because they carry the title of a Christian and I don't? What's the point of me getting saved?" This was how I used to think and I actually thought my explanations were valid because, again, my mind had not been renewed.

It wasn't until after I got saved that there was a change that took place in how I thought and what thoughts I allowed to cross my mind. I'm not saying that as soon as I rededicated my life back to Christ that every way I used to think or how I felt just instantly disappeared and ceased to no longer exist. But I do know that the more I allowed the Holy Spirit to move through me, the more the Father was able to change me. As I allowed my mind to be renewed, I gradually started moving from thinking out of the flesh to thinking through the Spirit. Meaning, I went from an old sinful way to thinking, to allowing God to change my thinking. Before I got saved, I had no problem with holding on to unforgiveness; but after I got saved, I understood that in order to be forgiven by God, I had to forgive others (Matthew 6:14). When I was out in the world, I had a sharp tongue. If you made me angry, I would cuss you out, tell you what I thought about you, and not think twice about it. But after my mind became renewed through Jesus, I learned how important it was to guard your tongue because that is where death and life lies (Proverbs 18:21).

As you now understand why renewing your mind is essential in living for God, carrying out what needs to be done to keep your mind renewed is just as significant. Maintaining a renewed mind is like your personal vehicle: in order for it to work, you have to keep it serviced. This includes everything from reading and studying God's Word daily (which I will discuss later) to praying and fasting (see Chapter 2). You will have a better understanding of what the Father has for you and how much He loves you because your thought process will be clearer. Having a renewed mind will result in you drawing closer to God, having a deeper relationship with Jesus, and allowing the Holy Spirit to lead you in every step of the way along life's journey.

Walking by Sight and Not by Faith

"For we walk by faith, not by sight."

— 2 CORINTHIANS 5:7 (ESV)

When we look at 2 Corinthians 5:7, Apostle Paul is encouraging the church at Corinth to walk by faith, not by sight. In this Scripture, the word *walk* pertains to how we are living the life that the Father has given us. It is a way to gauge what we are doing with the time we have left on this earth. It deals with trusting God and relying on His Word no matter what is going on within or around you. The more you choose to exercise your right to walk in faith, the stronger your walk with God will become.

There are so many in the Bible who chose to walk in faith for God. Noah operated in faith when God told him to build an ark. As a result of his obedience, Noah and his family were spared when a flood covered the whole earth. As an act of faith, Abraham left his native country, resulting in him becoming the father of many nations at an old age. Ruth, as an act of faith, chose to leave her country and follow her mother-in-law Naomi, married Boaz, and became the great-grandmother of a child who would later become a well-known, powerful ruler over Israel named David. These are just a few examples of the ones who chose to walk by faith. But what happens when you walk by sight instead of faith?

When a person chooses to walk by sight and not by faith, they move in their flesh instead of moving in the Spirit. They are choosing to operate in doubt, fear, and unbelief as a way to cope with what is in front of them. They become easily swayed by the obstacles and situations that appear bigger than themselves instead of choosing to stand in faith. Looking for reasons to complain becomes easier than looking for reasons to encourage others. This is not how the Father wants us to live our lives.

Just like there were people in the Bible who chose to move in faith, there were also some who chose to do the opposite. In Numbers 13-14, you will find the story about the twelve spies Moses sent to spy out the land of Canaan (Israel's Promised Land). For forty days, these men spied out the land of Canaan and after they were finished, they returned and told Moses, Aaron, and the children of Israel what they saw. Ten of the twelve spies came back with a negative report. They allowed what they saw to put fear in their hearts. They were able to successfully transfer that fear to the rest of the camp, and they caused the Israelites to cry and complain. Because of this, neither the ten spies nor the children of Israel were allowed to enter into the Promised Land. They ended up wandering in the wilderness for forty years (one year for each day they searched out the land) because they allowed fear to rule in their hearts instead of faith in God's promises for them. Joshua and Caleb were allowed to enter into the promised land because they were the only two spies who came back with a positive report and tried to encourage the children of Israel (Numbers 14:6-9).

Now can you see and understand why it is important to walk by faith and the repercussions of what happens when you choose to walk by sight? How will you choose to respond? When the reality isn't lining up with the revelation, will you still remain hopeful or become hopeless? Will you allow yourself to draw closer to the Father or will you try to get as far away from Him as you can because of what you are facing? Do not allow yourself to miss out on what God has for you by taking matters into your own hands. He knows the end from the beginning, and He can take you much further than you will ever know if you allow yourself to walk in faith and walk in His faithfulness. He is the author and finisher of our faith (Hebrews 12:2), so why not fully trust Him?

Not Reading the Word

In one of the sermons my bishop preached, I remember him saying, "You know, the best place to hide things from clueless people is in a book." This statement is both sad and true because the very questions or issues people have could be answered or resolved sooner than they think if they just take the time to research and read about what they are looking for or have need of. Yes, you can uncover so many things by reading **a book**, but what about the numerous things you could discover by reading **the Book** (the Bible)?

So many consequences could come from not reading God's Word. In Ephesians 6:11-17, Paul talked about how important it is to be dressed in the whole "Armor of God." Paul explained why this special armor is imperative to remain covered in:

> *"Put on the whole armor of God, that you may be able to stand against the schemes of the devil."*

> — EPHESIANS 6:11 (ESV)

In this passage of Scripture, Paul was not talking about actual pieces of armor. He used metaphors to express the significance of being equipped and protected against the schemes of the enemy so that you will not be ignorant of his devices (2 Corinthians 2:11). In the latter part of Ephesians 6:17, Paul talks about the sword of the Spirit being the Word of God. When you look at an actual sword, it is a weapon that is used to cut, sever, and destroy whatever it comes in contact with. It is used with the intent to cause harm and destruction. When the enemy tries to bring an attack against you (regardless of what form the attack comes in), it is the Word of God that will defend you and destroy the enemy, his demons, and his wicked devices. The doctor may give you a negative medical report, but you can combat that with God's Word and say, "By His (Jesus') stripes, I am healed" (Isaiah 53:5). Someone may try to bring up your past, but you can cut that down by saying, "I'm a new creation in Christ and because of that, old things have passed away, and a new thing has begun" (2 Corinthians 5:17).

This is how you defeat the enemy, but if you are not reading God's Word, you have no way of defending yourself. Contrary to popular belief, the enemy not only knows the Word of God, he also knows whether or not you know the Word of God. That's how he is able to defeat you by using the very Word against you that you choose not to read. So, if you are suffering from fear or constantly living in fear but you don't know what God's Word says about fear, the enemy will continue to destroy you with fear because you are not equipped to fight and win against him.

Another consequence of not reading God's Word is that it will cause you to become spiritually malnourished. When you think about physical food, it satisfies your hunger, it gives you energy, and it will keep you full until the next time you become hungry again. Imagine if you only ate once a week. What would be the outcome of your physical state? You would be starving, extremely malnourished, and probably close to the point of causing serious harm to your body. Not only can God's Word be used as a weapon, it is also a form of spiritual food. I just gave you the example of physically eating once a week, but what if I used it to describe being spiritually fed once a week? What if the only time you read your Bible was when you went to church once a week for service? Or even worse, what if you never read God's Word at all? Your spirit would be starving and you would not have the energy to make it through the day because you would not have the spiritual strength you need to make it and defend yourself against the attacks of the enemy.

Choosing not to read God's Word will also open doors in your life to be deceived and confused. There are so many things that are going on in the world today that go completely against what God says in His Word. We are now living in a day and age where right is wrong and wrong is right (Isaiah 5:20). This is a terrible state to be in because if you are not exposed to God's Word, you will believe that what you are doing, how you are acting, and how you choose to believe is the norm. You deserve much more than to walk through this life spiritually malnourished.

---

1. Fear. (n.d.). Retrieved January 23, 2018, from https://www.merriamweb ster.com/dictionary/fear
2. Fear. (n.d.). Retrieved January 23, 2018, from http://medical-dictionary.thefreedictionary.com/fear

2

REMOVING FEAR FROM YOUR LIFE

No matter who you are, everyone has experienced, is experiencing, or will experience fear in their life. These types of fears could range from the ones that are obvious to the ones that are holding you captive without you realizing it. Not dealing with fear could place you in a spiritual jail cell (bondage) that you were not created to be in. It could rob you of the peace and joy you were intended to have. This is important to understand so that you will know how to remove fear from your life so that you will be able to walk in the life that leads to fulfilling the purpose that God has for you.

How Do You Remove Fear?

In order to be set free (delivered) from fear, you must first know how to remove it. Knowing how to combat fear will not only set you free, it will also take you to higher levels in God. Some years back, I heard someone say that fear is false evidence appearing real (F.E.A.R.). It is something the enemy tries to present to you to weaken you or to drive you into further hopelessness. However, if you can remove the false evidence the enemy is trying to give to you, you can receive the truth that the Father has already given to you. So what are some ways you can remove the fear the enemy has placed on you?

Prayer

The simplest definition I can use to describe prayer is that it is a form of direct communication between you and God. It can be seen as a two-way conversation: you speak to the Father and He listens and in return, the Father speaks to you and you listen and obey. As powerful of a weapon as prayer is, some people use prayer as a last resort or they do not use it at all. Some people choose not to pray because it's seen as a waste of time or they do not have time to pray. Others choose not to pray because they do not see the value or the importance of it. This is unfortunate because prayer opens up so many doors for God to manifest in your life.

When you pray, you are inviting the Father to speak to you. As you seek Him in prayer, He will receive you. Prayer is an amazing tool that unlocks the answers you need, but it is not until you get before God and allow Him to speak to you that this will happen. So much can be done through prayer, but so many do not take advantage of it. When you elect not to pray to the Father, it's like tossing a beautiful pearl from an oyster back into the ocean. Prayer is worth so much, but so many see it as the opposite. Some may see prayer as a waste of time but in actuality, it is time well spent. It is not until you fully and completely release yourself over to the Father that He can hear from you and what you have on your heart.

So how does prayer remove fear? In order for fear to be removed from your life, you must first be willing to release your fears over to God. Philippians 4:6-7 (NLT) says, *"Don't worry about anything; instead, pray about everything. Tell God what you need, and thank him for all he has done. Then you will experience God's peace, which exceeds anything we can understand. His peace will guard your hearts and minds as you live in Christ Jesus."* As you seek God and pray to Him about your fears, He will give you peace in exchange for your fears. God did not create you to live in fear. He created you to enjoy a life that is full of abundance. The way to enjoying a life full of abundance is *"by casting all your cares on him because he cares for you"* (1 Peter 5:7, NETB). You can be set free from the bondage of fear and live in the fullness of Christ's freedom. It is here, you will be able to receive what God has for you and so much more.

Reading God's Word

"For the word of God is living and active. Sharper than any double-edged sword, it pierces even to dividing soul and spirit, joints and marrow. It is able to judge the thoughts and intentions of the heart."

— HEBREWS 4:12 (BSB)

The living Word is knowing that God is alive and His Word will never be able to be pulled away from Him. His Word will always remain. Not only is God's Word alive, it can also give new life. God's Word can cause "dead things" to come alive and flourish within and all around you. Plenty of times, I felt like God was far away from me because of what I had to go through and what I had to face or from me not spending the time with Him that I should have. However, when I allowed myself to draw closer to God's Word, I was able to receive the reconnection from His heart that I needed.

God's Word can restore and bring new hope into every area of your life that needs to be revived. It can speak to any circumstance or situation and provide you with the comfort, growth, and healing that you need. No matter how old the Bible may be, there is no such thing as expiration when it comes to new revelation of God's Word. Scriptures in the Bible were written centuries ago, but they are still relevant for what we encounter in current times today. You will always be able to receive new insight from God's Word because the Holy Spirit is speaking through it.

God's talks about fear throughout the Bible so if someone is not searching out how to combat fear, they will continue to be destroyed by it. The enemy knows the Word just like we do or as we should know it. If you do not read God's Word and allow yourself to become immersed in it, he (the enemy) knows how to use the Word against you. Therefore, if a person is constantly in fear and not reading God's Word on how to combat it, they will continue to remain in fear because they are neglecting to grab hold of the revelation that the Father has for them. Some of the benefits for reading God's Word are:

You Will Not Fall for Satan's Temptations

The more you read God's Word, the more you will become aware of what is considered right and wrong. This is important because every time the enemy tries to get you to sin against God, you will have the power and authority to speak God's Word against him. As you become more immersed in God's Word it will become harder for the enemy to tempt you because you have allowed God's Word to become an anchor inside of you so that you will not become shaken by what the enemy tries to use as a form of deception against you.

You Will Begin to Know God Better

As you allow yourself to connect more to God's Word, you will start to become familiar with who God is, how He feels about you, and the promises that He has in store for you. The more time you spend in God's Word, the more you will be able to hear from Him, and by doing so, you will begin to build up your intimacy and establish a relationship with Him. As you get to know the Father better, you can connect more to His heart and be in tune with what He has to say to you and how He feels about you.

You Will Learn About Jesus

Jesus is the Son of the most High God. He was sent to earth by God to be a sacrifice for all mankind so that we could be restored back to the Father by receiving Jesus Christ. In the four gospels of the Bible (Matthew, Mark, Luke, and John), you can read different stories that talk about everything from the birth of Jesus (being born of a virgin) to some of His miracles and healings that were recorded, His betrayal and crucifixion, and His resurrection and ascension back to heaven. Jesus has a love that expresses the multitude of His heart because of the longing He has for God's creation to be restored back to Him forever; reading God's Word will give you a glimpse of how Jesus adores you.

Fasting

Fasting comes with the rejection of something (food most commonly) for a certain amount of time as a way to increase and direct our attention towards God so that He can operate more in our lives. Fasting is an important aspect for spiritual growth. The true heart of spiritual discipline (especially for Christians) can be found in fasting. It is a sure way to align our hearts with the heart of God so that we can hear what He has to say to us. Prayer and fasting work best together. When these two methods are combined, it leads to a gateway the Holy Spirit uses to change your life.

When viewed from a biblical perspective, fasting is something that can be seen as high importance, gainful, and valuable. Throughout the Bible, you can read about people who declared fasts before something had to be decided on, when they were in need of revelation, or when they were facing problems or oppositions.

Why is Fasting Important?

When done in proper order and for the right reasons, fasting can move you to higher levels in many areas of your life. When used with Scripture, a willing desire, and a humble, submissive heart to seek God, fasting will break through so many barriers in the spirit realm and cause breakthroughs to take place in the natural realm. Through fasting and prayer, the Father will hear you where you are and start healing in areas of your life, your family, others who are connected to you, your church, your city/community, your nation, and even the world. Fasting is needed so that God can change the hearts of those who want to go deeper in Him. Some important reasons to fast are as follows:

To Follow the Example of Jesus

When it comes to fasting, Jesus is the best example to follow. In Matthew 4:1-11, you can read about how Jesus was tempted by Satan after He had completed a 40-day fast. For every temptation the enemy tried to use against Jesus, He destroyed them with the Word of God. Fasting for 40 days and 40 nights was what gave Jesus the anointing and power He needed to resist Satan's enticements. Because Jesus was able to overcome all of Satan's temptations, He started a ministry that consisted of numerous miracles and healings.

God's Purpose and Direction for You Will be Revealed

While fasting in January 2016, the Father downloaded so much revelation into my spirit that it was amazingly overwhelming to me! God wanted me to make a list of every question that I wanted Him to give me revelation about; one of the questions I had was about a new job.

A year prior to this fast, I had just retired from the military after serving for 15 years. The details of me being forced into early retirement from the military are discussed in a book anthology I was featured in titled *"You Have No Idea the Hell I've Been Through: 22 Women Who Pushed from Pain to Purpose"* (www.youhavenoideabooks.com). In July 2015, I started working for the federal government. Initially, I was excited because I saw this move as a fresh start but by the second day, I was ready to jump ship. I ended up working in an organization that was dysfunctional, toxic, and unprofessional. I was overworked, unappreciated, and tried to find an exit out by looking and applying for other jobs daily. I was miserable; I wanted out and fast! I knew eventually I was going to leave, but the way I thought I was going to leave was completely different from how I actually left, which brings me to January 2016.

In January 2016, one of the things I sought God on while I was fasting was the specifics for a new job. When I was offered the job at this organization, I didn't seek God on it first. I just accepted the job and because of that, I wanted to make sure that I had His approval for the next place I would work because I didn't want to make the same mistake twice. When I sought the Father for revelation about my next job, He told me not to waste any more time looking for jobs because the assignment He had for me was going to be my next job. I'm thinking to myself, *Wait, what?* He then goes on to tell me that I was going to stop working that same year and **start** working for Him! As of this point, I couldn't believe what I was hearing!

And if that wasn't enough, God told me what He was calling me to do: To be an author, writer, and speaker for women around the world to encourage and inspire them with the words that He gives me to write and speak. He gave me the name for my businesses, the vision and mission statements, and so many other things! Then I finally knew what my purpose was. I finally knew why the Father sent me to this earth, and it made me feel good. I was absolutely amazed at what He was revealing to me, but I was even more amazed at how fast it all happened!

Six months after God gave me this revelation, I resigned from my job. Two months after I resigned from my job, I got my business license for Faith Led Life and Faith Led Life Coaching, LLC. In April 2017, I launched my website (www.-faithledlife.com). About three months after launching my website, I started working on my first manuscript and then the second manuscript (this book) the following month. The same month I started working on my second manuscript, I was selected to be featured in the anthology I mentioned above. This is only the beginning by the way! I'm looking forward to seeing even greater things that God has in store for me, and you should too! God is so awesome with the way He does things! We may have our plans laid out, but He has a way of directing and/or redirecting us in the way we should go that is destined to lead us to His purpose. And just think, all of this came about when I made a decision to fast.

Deliverance Will Come

God asked a question in Isaiah 58:6 (NIV): *"Is not this the kind of fasting I have chosen: to loose the chains of injustice and untie the cords of the yoke, to set the oppressed free and break every yoke?"* Whether it's an addiction, a bad habit, or some form of bondage, deliverance will come when fought the right way. When God's Word is used while fasting, you have just made the choice to use a combination that the enemy will not be able to stand against. Matthew 4:1-11 is the example I would like to use again to demonstrate this. When Jesus had finished His 40-day fast, Satan immediately came and tempted Him. Satan tried three different ways, but Jesus' defense was the same: the use of God's Word. Choosing to use God's Word as a weapon was how Jesus was able to defeat the enemy, and that opened the door for us to do the same thing.

Different Ways to Fast

There are different types of fasts you can choose to do, but the one you allow God to choose for you is the one that He will see as a true sacrifice. I would also like to add that if you just focus on the food and continue on with your regular routine of doing things but do not set aside time to the read God's Word, pray, praise and worship Him, and go deeper with seeking Him, you're not fasting, you're dieting. Some of the ways you can fast are as follows:

- Total Fast or Full Fast: When you give up all foods and drinks for an extended period of time.
- Water Fast: When you give up all foods but only drink water for an extended period of time.

- Liquid Fast: When you give up all foods but you only drink water, juices, or other natural liquids (broth) for an extended period of time.
- Partial Fast: When you select certain times of the day to fast [6:00AM-6:00PM, 6:00PM-6:00AM, or however you choose to select your time or time of the day (morning-afternoon, afternoon-evening, evening-night)] for an extended period of time.

The Importance of Fasting Against Fear

Fasting is when you deny your flesh. When you choose to deny your flesh (or whatever it is that you're coming to the Father about) and you go before God with a need, there's nothing distracting you. He has your attention so therefore, He can speak to you and you can clearly hear from Him in regards to what you are coming to Him about. So, if you are coming to God about fear, your attention is on Him. Fasting is when you go a length of time without eating or you have eating restrictions. This is how Adam and Eve fell. They ate fruit from a tree they were told by God not to eat from (Genesis 2:16-17). Resisting your flesh is how you are able to stand firm. Resisting what you want for a greater need in order for a breakthrough to take place is why fasting is important.

Meditating

If you are trying to progress in your personal and spiritual development but fear is stopping you from doing so, meditating on God's Word is how you will be able to break free from that. Meditating allows God's thoughts to replace our thoughts. Meditating on God's Word will remove the fear that is trying to stop you from moving forward in life. If allowed to, fear will try to make you become stagnant to the point that you will not be able to walk in your purpose. Fear will distort the worries in your mind and use it to present an unwanted result.

For instance, if you are afraid of the dark, you will more than likely be prone to believe that something or someone will be waiting to attack you. Someone who is fearful of dogs may think that every dog they see wants to bite them. Someone may desire to start their own business but they choose not to because they are afraid that their business will be unsuccessful. Who knows whether these scenarios will actually happen but sometimes we have a tendency to believe the pictures we create in our minds and hold them as truth when in actuality, they are not. This is the false evidence appearing real that I was talking about earlier - believing something that appears real without having the tangible evidence to back it up.

When you choose to implement meditation as part of your life, it confronts the worries and anxieties that you may have by getting rid of the harmful picture that comes from fear and substitutes it with the assurances that are found in the Father's Word. When your mindset has been redirected, you will be able to stand boldly and conquer fear by taking the necessary steps to come against it.

For example, you have a serious fear of speaking to others. You want to become more engaged with people but something as simple as saying hello stops you from moving any further. One day before leaving your house, you say to yourself, "Today, I'm going to speak to three people I don't know."

You are out at a public place and you see someone walking in your direction. You are completely aware of what you said moments earlier when you were home but fear has now grabbed hold of you and because of this, you run into the nearest department store just to avoid speaking to a stranger. To defeat the fear of speaking to people, meditate on 2 Timothy 1:7 (KJV) which says, *"For God hath not given us the spirit of fear; but of power, and of love, and of a sound mind."*

When you meditate on Scriptures that deal with fear, it's like medicine: it heals you from the inside out. You're filling yourself with spiritual medicine so the more of it you take (by reading God's Word), the better you will feel. That spirit will no longer hold you captive because you are spiritually medicating yourself with the Father's Word.

3

WHEN FAITH ISN'T ENOUGH

"So also faith alone without works is dead."

— JAMES 2:17 (ABPE)

Activating Your Faith

Faith in God alone is not enough. You can have knowledge of something and not have trust in what you know. Someone can believe that Jesus lived on this earth, was crucified, and rose from the dead but not allow what they believe to go any further than that. The reason why is because they are not allowing what they believe to line up with what they should be doing. If a person claims to have faith, the works (actions) of that person should reflect that.

Salvation is deliverance from sin and its consequences and believed by Christians to be brought about by faith in Jesus Christ. [1]When you put your trust in Jesus, salvation will come. In doing so, we will be made over to the point of where we will start to make decisions that are original and diverse for the glory of God. When you decide to live and operate in faith, you are giving God permission to change the path of your life. As you move in faith, you will also be moved to begin to do works, good works, that abide in the heart and the will of the Father. Otherwise in choosing not to do so, you will not have works, just "dead faith" that comes from words only.

Please do not mistake what I'm saying. I'm not saying that in order for you to receive salvation, you have to do good works, live a perfect life, and obey the laws. I am saying that doing good works that are a result of obeying God is what those who trust in Jesus will start to do. It is faith in Jesus that will deliver and save you, and the same faith that delivers and saves you is the same faith that will cause good works to come out of you.

The Season I Had to Activate My Faith

This overall process of me walking in my calling was an act of faith. I retired from the military in 2015 because I was blackballed and went through being racially and sexually discriminated against. As a Christian serving in the military, there were things that I refused to tolerate and go along with, especially compromising who I was as God's daughter, because of the type of toxic units I was in. Because I was blackballed, I was forced to retire early which caused my military career to be cut short. The act of faith began while I was transitioning out of the military.

When I was close to the end of my military career, the Father told me that I was going to move to Northern Virginia. About seven months after I retired, I relocated to the exact city where God said I was going to live (I had never lived in Virginia nor did I know anything about the city He told me about) and got a job as a federal government worker on a military installation. While embarking on this new territory, God sent prophetic people in my life and started telling me that I was going to become a blogger, author, and speaker. The acts of faith continued to kick in when God told me to resign from the federal government system. For me, it was hard to get employed by the federal government but I clearly heard God tell me to resign from my job. After 11 months into working for the federal government and out of obedience to the Father, I resigned from my job to do what I am doing today-impacting the lives of women all around the world.

For some of you who are reading this, you're probably saying, "Wow, I don't think I could have done that." During certain parts of the process, I didn't want to either (I'm just being transparent). When the Father initially told me about all of this, I wasn't like, *OK, God, I'll do it!* I had questions. I had concerns. I had **FEARS**.

For a long time, I did not want this assignment because I was afraid of losing, I was afraid of failing, and I was afraid to step out on faith because of the things I thought I lacked. I wanted to work on my job longer so that I could make more money to get the things started that God needed me to do. However, the Father told me that I would have never made enough money to start working for Him because the plans He has for me far exceed any amount of money on this earth

I could ever make, and I had to believe that. He went on further to tell me, *"I would never give you an assignment that matches your bank account, where's the faith in that? If that was the case, you would be doing it out of your own strength instead of Me doing it for you."*

Hearing the Father tell me all of this initially came as a hard pill to swallow, but I knew that it was something that I needed to hear. I needed Him to tell me that I had to believe in Him. I needed Him to tell me that He really did have great plans for me. He operates in ways that do not make sense to us, but it makes perfect sense to Him because it lines up with His will. I was convicted so I finally chose to come under His submission and resign from my federal government job to walk in the purpose and calling He has me doing today which is to write, speak, and be a Christian life coach for women.

Bound by Discouragement

Have you ever received a word from God? Initially, you're happy and excited about the revelation you have received. But over time, it seems like it's taking forever for that word to come to pass. You know what God has told you but when it doesn't happen when you think it should, you become discouraged. You choose to keep your faith bound or suppressed when you allow the enemy to cause you to question what God has already answered. If not careful, you could discourage yourself out of your blessings whether it's due to impatience or choosing to focus on what you see instead of what you know.

There has been some point in life where we all have experienced discouragement. Discouragement is one of the most common ways the enemy infiltrates into people's lives. Discouragement has the ability to enter into someone's life when they don't have the knowledge of God at that moment, which can lead a person to operate out of emotion. Operating out of emotion is exactly what the enemy wants you to do because when you do, he can now cause you to exaggerate how you are feeling due to what you are experiencing. This is why activating your faith is important. Just like light and darkness can't dwell in the same place at the same time, neither can worry and faith. If you choose to worry, there will be no room for faith to come in; if you choose to operate in faith, worry has no choice but to leave.

There are so many ways the enemy can cause discouragement to enter into someone's life. One of the ways he is successful at doing this is by causing people to sabotage themselves. They speak discouragement over themselves instead of speaking what brings life, which is the Word of God. They could talk about God and His promises, but they choose to talk about their problems and situations instead. This is how seeds of fear are planted inside of you, resulting in you not receiving the harvest of life.

Discouraged people have a tendency to gravitate towards others who are discouraged because as the saying goes, "Misery loves company." They will cling to each other more as a way to justify their reason for being in that state. Others who are on the outside of this "discouraging circle" may try to reach out to help but could get refused for some reason. However, when a person inside of the circle finally taps into the goodness of Jesus, they now want to break away from that negative circle they have allowed themselves to be entangled by and cling more to the peace and comfort that the Father has for them.

Discouragement is how the enemy is able to keep you bound; being bound is how fear is able to come into your life. When you choose to operate in fear, you have just allowed it to override the power and authority that God has for you to receive. It will be disappointing to allow fear to position itself in your life and take away the faith that God has available for you. But as you submit more to the Holy Spirit, fear will no longer be able to take hold of you. Instead of having fear live inside of you, God's love can abide in you because as 1 John 4:18 (ESV) says, *"There is no fear in love, but perfect love casts out fear. For fear has to do with punishment, and whoever fears has not been perfected in love."*

Going Through the Motions: Getting Comfortable in Your Ways

Going through the motions can disrupt the liveliness of faith. It can bring you to a place of standing still when God wants you to keep moving forward. If not careful, being comfortable where you are in your faith could lead to unforeseen obstacles ahead. When this happens, we deprive ourselves of the Father's power and help because we stop relying on Him and depend more on ourselves. Now if you being comfortable causes you to rely on God, then that's great. But if it's causing you to become complacent, you could miss out on some serious things that God wants you to do pertaining to Him.

How I Allowed Comfort to Hold Me Hostage

I got comfortable when God was telling me that I was going to become an author and a speaker. He was ready for me to start when He wanted me to, but I wasn't ready - or so I thought. I allowed a few things to kick in. I allowed perfectionism to kick in by telling myself, *I don't have a website yet. I need to get my pictures taken for my website. I don't have a domain name yet.* I felt as if I had to have all these things in line and set up before I stepped out and did what He wanted me to do or what He was calling me to do. This led to more perfectionism and procrastination but overall, it was fear. I was coming up with excuses as to why I could not get started because of things I felt I needed but the Father kept telling me, *"You start where you are; I'll add to what you need."* But for a long time, I wasn't grasping what He was saying.

In 2016 during a New Year's Eve celebration at my church, strips of paper were handed out to everybody. Close to the end of the service, my bishop told everyone to take the paper and write down three things we did not want to bring into 2017. Without hesitation, I wrote down perfectionism, procrastination, and fear of walking in my purpose and calling. After everybody had finished writing, the ushers collected our papers and threw them in trashcans that were at the front of the sanctuary. My bishop then stretched his hands over them and prayed for the curses to be broken off everyone based on what we had written down. And since then, everything I said I couldn't do, I was now doing. I was no longer making excuses because they weren't working. If there was something that I needed to do and I was afraid, I did it anyway because I was on assignment.

You will never get anywhere if you never move your feet. These were the faith steps that I had to take to get moving. Your steps may be the same as mine or they may be different. It doesn't matter how you start, just start.

---

1. (n.d.). Retrieved January 23, 2018, from https://www.google.com/search?q=Dictionary#dobs=salvation

4

HIDING BEHIND THE CROSS

"So we tell others about Christ, warning everyone and teaching everyone with all the wisdom God has given us. We want to present them to God, perfect in their relationship to Christ."

— COLOSSIANS 1:28 (NLT)

We have the opportunity of involving ourselves with the Father in the completion of His Great Commission through the present generation. One of the ways changes can take place in the world is when the change first takes place in us. The more this happens, the more will take place in our homes, our jobs, our schools, our communities, our churches, our nation, and around the world for the better. We do not have the power to change anybody in this world, Jesus is the only One who can do that, but we can come together to transform the world by presenting Jesus to others.

Revelation of the Cross: How to Present Jesus on the Cross to the Unbeliever Without Fear

If you are going to minister to unbelievers, you need to think like you're going to another country you've never been to before. You're going to a place where everyone speaks a different language than you, they're not familiar with your culture, and you have to leave from where you are to bring them to where they need to be. Immediately, there are some assumptions you automatically know that you wouldn't make: You wouldn't believe that just because you landed in this country that everybody should instantly know who you are. You wouldn't convince yourself that just because you're passionate about what you have to say that everyone else should feel the same way as well. And you certainly wouldn't assume that they should already know that they must have forgiveness from God. The reality of the matter is that you don't have to go to another country where Jesus is unheard of or not believed in. When it comes to this topic, there are people in our own country who do not speak the same "spiritual language" we do.

Presenting Jesus to unbelievers is important, but how you present Jesus can be helpful or harmful. Prior to you presenting Jesus to unbelievers, you have to:

1. Make sure that you are actually a Christian, not just in name only.

Christian is a word that is used for someone who believes in Jesus Christ. However, there is much more to being a Christian than just saying, "I'm a Christian." One of the most important steps a Christian can take is repentance. When a person repents, it goes much deeper than having an "emotional moment," it is a life-changing action. Repentance will stop you from where you are going spiritually and take you in a different direction for the better. You will truly be sorry for the sins that you commit to the point of where you no longer want to commit them.

Being a Christian also requires being willing to fully surrender and completely give your life to God. You have to be willing to give up yourself in order to be able to grab hold of what God has for you and what He needs for you to do for Him. There's an expensive price that comes with being a Christian. It consists of having a full commitment and obligation to the Father. There will be times when you fall along this Christian journey, but God will always be there to help you stand back up so that you can keep walking. You have to allow Him to be first in all areas of your life and completely depend on Him.

2. Make sure the Holy Spirit is a part of your life.

The moment we accept Jesus as our Savior, we receive salvation, and from that moment on, the Holy Spirit lives inside of us. The reason why the Holy Spirit is living inside of us is so that we can become equipped and empowered by Him. As you cultivate a relationship with the Holy Spirit, you will begin to be more in tune in ways you never thought possible. When you find yourself struggling with sin or temptation, the Holy Spirit will give you the Scripture you need at the exact moment you need it to overcome what the enemy is trying to place before you. When you find yourself in prayer and you need answers or guidance, the Holy Spirit will give you the revelation that you need. Allowing the Holy Spirit to dwell in you will prepare you for God's service and put a boldness in you that will propel you for the glory of God's Kingdom.

Below are a few suggestions that will assist you with introducing unbelievers to Christ:

- **Prayer.** Start the day off with prayer, and make sure that it includes you petitioning the Holy Spirit to equip you as well as lead you to the ones whose hearts He has already prepared to receive Him.
- **Be relatable.** Do not approach unbelievers in a way that seems aggressive or emotionless. Present yourself in a way that seems approachable, caring, and natural. The more you grow in Jesus, the more you will be able to walk in His love and when this happens, those whom you are sharing Christ with will see that you are real. They will be able to see that you are not trying to approach them with a hidden agenda but that you are taking time to speak to them because of the love of God that is living inside of you.
- Just so that you know in advance, not everybody is going to be receptive with receiving and accepting Jesus. They may respond to you in a negative way whether it comes out in their actions or their words. If this does happen, do not become discouraged and do not respond out of your flesh. You may have been the one the Father wanted to be the first to plant that seed in their heart, but he may have other messengers lined up to nurture His Word more and more until the harvest (the individual finally

accepting Christ) is ready to manifest. However it turns out, just allow the Holy Spirit to lead with whatever it is He wants you to do.

- **Keep it simple.** Don't try to get too technical with ministering to an unbeliever. Everybody is not where you are and because of that, some will not be able to understand what you are saying if you try to talk to them in a way they can't comprehend. Let them know how much God loves them. Tell them that if they were the only person living on the earth, God still would've sent His Son to die for them. Give them the moral meaning behind certain stories from the Bible without leaving them confused; or better yet, tell them stories (or give them Scriptures) that are relatable to what they are facing at the moment. Step out on faith even more and give them your testimony about where you once were, who you used to be, and how God delivered you. If the unbeliever is ready to continue, they will confess and repent of their sins, accept Jesus Christ as their Savior, and confess Him as Lord over their life. These are the steps you take in introducing and sharing Jesus without fear.

Many People Are Hiding Behind Fear Instead of Faith

I have some important news for you today: the Father wants you to stop focusing on the fears in your life. Anytime His children walk in fear, they are not walking according to His will and purpose. The Father wants you to keep your thoughts moving forward and not allow fear to paralyze you. Fear will stop you from reaching your highest levels in God. It will stop you from moving forward in faith and cause you to believe what is in front of you (or what you are facing) is bigger than a God who has given you the power to conquer it. The enemy has a tendency of inflicting fear on God's people to stop them from moving forward. If the enemy can stop you from moving, he can stop you from reaching the destination that God is sending you to. If he can keep you in fear, he can cause you to doubt yourself, your goals, your passion, and even God - this is a strong desire the enemy has. If the enemy can cause you to doubt God, he can cause you to doubt every promise He has for you and made to you.

So where does fear come from? Second Timothy 1:7 says, *"For God did not give us a spirit of fear, but of power and of love and of a sound mind"* (NKJV). Fear is what the enemy imposes on you as an attempt to stop you from destroying his schemes and works. If he can keep your mind on fear, your mind is no longer focused on the Father.

So many women operate out of fear and they don't even realize it. They may not come out and say that they are fearful about a certain issue or situation, but their response to it speaks volumes. A woman could live in fear that she is going to spend the rest of her life alone or die alone; because fear is now ringing in her ear louder than the voice of God, she ends up in a relationship/marriage that causes her more harm than good. A woman who is a single parent could live in fear believing that she doesn't have enough money to provide for her children, so she goes out and either gets multiple jobs or constantly works extended hours on one job to make more money. But while she's gaining more income for her household, her children are lacking attention or feeling unloved or unwanted. Or what about the woman who is so fearful of losing her husband, she conforms to his requests, expectations (whether right/wrong, good/bad), and how he thinks she should be while losing her identity in the process. But do you know what the opposite of fear is? It's faith.

Hebrews 11:1 (KJV) describes faith as *"the substance of things hoped for, the evidence of things not seen."* Faith is believing God's promises for you when the reality isn't lining up with the revelation. It is being able to see the end while you are still living in the beginning of your story. It means to own something in advance before you possess it in the natural. Earlier, I gave some examples of how fear can override faith, but Mark 5:25-34 shows us what happens when faith is placed over fear.

This story revolves around a woman who had a prolonged, uncontrollable issue of blood for 12 years. This means from the time she woke up to the time she went to sleep (and even while she was sleeping), this bleeding flowed like water from her body. She was seen by numerous doctors during that time, but none of them were able to help her; so instead of her getting better, she got worse. All the money that she had was now gone due to her attempts to get this issue resolved but little did she know, she was about to encounter the Great Physician Himself.

In this passage, Jesus is surrounded by a lot of people. He was trying to get past the crowd because a synagogue ruler named Jairus begged Him to come to his house and lay hands on his dying 12-year-old daughter. As Jesus was passing by, the woman heard about Him and what He had done and although she knew that His healing record spoke for itself, she was now faced with another problem. Because the crowd was closely surrounding Jesus, the woman did not have direct access to Him. This meant she had to pass through the crowd from behind in order to reach Jesus. There will be times in your life when you have to press through your problems, situations, and circumstances in order to reach the blessings that God has for you, especially when you know that He has already promised them to you.

In spite of all of the people, this woman was able to touch Jesus' garment because she said to herself, "If I just touch his clothes, I will be healed." She had enough faith to believe that touching the Savior's clothes would heal her. But you know what? She was right. Immediately after she touched Jesus' garment, the woman's bleeding stopped and just like that, she was healed. But here's where it gets interesting: when the woman touched Jesus, He felt power leave Him; while He was still standing within the crowd, Jesus turned around and asked, "Who touched me?" Now if the disciples were presently living today, their response probably would've been, "Come on, Jesus. You see all of these people touching You, grabbing You, throwing themselves at You and You want to know WHO touched You, really?"

Jesus started scanning the crowd to see who it was that caused power to leave Him. When the woman realized that she had been healed as a result of touching Jesus and probably knew that He was looking for her, she fell before Him and told Him everything that happened. Jesus did not scorn or humiliate this woman for what she did. He did not respond in a hateful or offensive manner towards her. Instead, He responded by saying, *"Daughter, your faith has healed you. Go in peace and be freed from your suffering"* (Mark 5:34, NIV). Because of an act of faith, she was healed and restored. But what if she would have operated in fear? What if she chose not to act on her faith? What if she would've told herself, "All these people are already crowding Him, so I'm not going to try to touch Him." What if she never admitted that she was the one who touched Jesus?

This woman gave a beautiful demonstration of what faith over fear looks like. She did not allow anything (not even her illness) or anyone to stop her from reaching the Savior; you have to feel the same way. No matter what your issue is or how bad it seems, don't ever allow fear to override your faith. Even when what you are facing seems overwhelming, have faith to believe in God anyway.

I pray that you will not live in fear but instead, live in the faith He has given you. You cannot allow the enemy to stop you from reaching the Father because of fear because if you do, you will not be able to receive the blessings He has for you. If you take one step of faith, God will take the rest of the steps for you and lead you to where you need to be - living fearlessly for Him.

5

REACHING FOR A HIGHER ANOINTING

"And as for you, the anointing which you received from Him abides in you, and you have no need for anyone to teach you, but as His anointing teaches you about all things, and is true and is not a lie, and just as it has taught you, you abide in Him."

— 1 JOHN 2:27 (NASB1995)

What is the Anointing?

The anointing can take place in two ways: either physically or spiritually. Some of the definitions for the physical are as follows:

- To rub or sprinkle on; apply an unguent, ointment, or oily liquid to.
- To smear with any liquid.
- To consecrate or make sacred in a ceremony that includes the token applying of oil.

- To dedicate to the service of God.[1]

From a spiritual perspective (which is what will be discussed for the rest of this chapter), the anointing is seeing the presence of God in manifestation and as we see God manifest, we will then see more supernatural things take place. God's anointing is on those who move in His supernatural powers. The anointing is the Father's way of giving you special access to allow Him to change the atmosphere around you, to do things through you, and to complete your assignment for Him.

Understanding the Anointing

Because of the times that we are living in, it's important that we have the anointing of God within us because it is something that Christians can operate in but the world cannot. The use of the word anointing is so loosely spoken in many churches, but not all Christians are comprehending what it really means; but as you receive more of a revelation about it, you will be able to correctly walk in the Father's anointing from that moment on.

The reason why you have the anointing of God is so that you represent Him. Being anointed does not make you better, more spiritual, or more blessed than anyone else. When you are seeking God for more of His anointing, make sure you realize what you are asking for because as the saying goes, "There's a cost that comes with the anointing," and it's a price that will cost you more than what you realize. When you are truly walking in the anointing of God, it's no longer about you. The more of the Father's anointing you receive, the more responsibilities you will not only have for God but for others as well. The more advanced the anointing becomes in your life, the more advanced the issues of the people around you will become so that God can use you to bring about the solution for them.

There are so many churches in which the leaders are able to talk about the anointing, but little to none of these churches experience the fullness of the Father's anointing and the ability to flow in the supernatural. In John 14:12 (NIV), Jesus said, *"Very truly I tell you, whoever believes in me will do the works I have been doing, and they will do even greater things than these, because I am going to the Father."* If Jesus spoke out of His own mouth that we will be able to do greater works than what He did, why is there little to any manifestation of this taking place today? Why are we not able to experience the fullness of the supernatural so that the breakthroughs, blessings, miracles, and healings can come and yokes and strongholds can be destroyed? Those who are around you should be able to see and witness God's anointing on your job, in your marriage, in your finances, in your church, within you, etc. If we were ever able to understand God and the power He wants us to receive, our dreams would explode out of the small box that we are trying to keep them suppressed in. If we could go beyond the four walls of our limitations, we would be able to flow freely in God's anointing.

Levels of Anointing

When you give your life to Christ and you are walking in the ways of God, the different levels of the anointing that you can operate in are:

Beginners' Level

This is the level where you give your life to Christ and you are known as a "babe in Christ." At this level, you are going through a transitional phase from the old person you used to be to allowing God to change you into the new person you will become. You no longer have a desire to do the things you used to do. The things that you thought were pleasurable before you got saved, you are now disgusted by the thought of them. The Father is providing for you and feeding you the spiritual nourishment that you need so that you will be able to grow stronger in Him. Even though you are not mature in God's Word, you know there's a feeling in you that's indescribable and you know you feel different but in a good way.

Intermediate Level

At this level, more evidence of the Father's presence is obvious in your life. You now have faith that goes beyond that of what you can see. You have it made up in your mind that you are under full submission to Jesus and you are living by the principles that God has before you. It is at this level that you invite the Holy Spirit to become more active in and around you. This also depends on where you are in your walk as far as what you are doing (or not doing) that will determine how fast or slow you will move in God. This will depend on things like the amount of time you spend fasting and praying to God, if you are saturating yourself in His Word, if you are putting God above everything and everyone else (including yourself), if you are in a church where the Spirit of the Lord is invited to move freely, etc. If you are lacking in these areas or others, it will definitely affect your spiritual growth process, which could result in you getting bored in your Christian walk, becoming complacent, or possibly walking away from God altogether.

Highest Level

This is the level where it's natural for the Holy Spirit to flow supernaturally in your life. Your faith is in overload and you are at a point in your life where you don't hope, you expect and believe in the miracles of God to take place in your life and the lives of others. You believe in the power of prayer, fasting will go from being a chore to you being excited about making the sacrifice for God, and your faith will take you places you never thought would be possible. Matthew 7:7-8 (ESV) says, *"Ask, and it will be given to you; seek, and you will find; knock, and it will be opened to you. For everyone who asks receives, and the one who seeks finds, and to the one who knocks it will be opened."* If you ask the Father for His anointing, or more of His anointing, He will give it to you. He wants you to receive His anointing more than ever, especially if it is during a moment in your life when He wants to give blessings to you. This is why it's important to have an intimate relationship with the Father so that you will not miss out on the blessings that He has for you.

How Do You Receive God's Anointing?

In some churches, there is a serious dispute in regards to the meaning of being anointed and who is considered anointed. As you read the Old Testament, you will read about how there were priests and kings who were anointed with oil as a form of consecration (being sanctified or set apart). However, when it comes with the new covenant that we have, this means that the Holy Spirit is living in us. The reason why we are anointed is so that we will be equipped to do God's work. So how are we able to receive God's anointing?

Make room in your life to receive God's anointing. There is something that the Holy Spirit has been telling you to let go of that you insist on holding on to. He has pricked your heart and convicted you about this time and time again, but you still have a hard time releasing yourself from it. What has the Holy Spirit been telling you to let go of? Has He been telling you to let go of the unforgiveness and bitterness that you have been carrying around in your heart towards the person or people who have hurt you in the past or present? Do you find yourself holding onto low self-esteem or believing that you lack worth? What about the temptation or struggle that you think you'll never be able to break free from? Are you operating in fear instead of living in faith?

Although these are different examples I just gave, they all come down to one thing: they are distractions placed in front of you to keep your attention away from God. The more you allow yourself to become distracted by whatever form that "distraction" may come in, the less room there will be for God's anointing to move through you. So, if you want to receive more of the Father's anointing, you have to be willing to let go of the things that He is trying to release you from so that you will be able to grab hold of more of the anointing that He wants to give to you - it's just that simple. As you allow yourself to be purged through the cleansing of the Holy Spirit, you will begin to receive God's anointing over your life.

By having faith in Jesus. Everyone receives God's anointing the moment they accept Jesus as their Savior. This is because as soon as a person gives their life to Christ, the Holy Spirit immediately abides in them. It is through the Holy Spirit that believers are spiritually trained because it is the Holy Spirit who will always lead you in the right direction, but please do not mistake what I'm saying. Knowing that the Holy Spirit will lead and guide you is not an invitation for believers to stop reading their Bibles, listening to leaders who teach biblical truth, or receiving godly advice. It means that because you know that the Holy Spirit is living in you, you will be able to be on one accord with other Christians who believe that God's Word is truth. As you continue to make the choice to remain in the presence of Jesus, you are making the decision to hold onto the anointing that comes with Him.

By sharing the gospel. More of the anointing can be received so that Christians will be able to share more of the gospel. The anointing of the Holy Spirit is needed for everything that we do, even when we tell others about Him and Jesus Christ. When we share the gospel, we are allowing the Holy Spirit to move through us to encourage others, to speak God's Word, and to operate more in a manner of discipleship and evangelism.

There are so many men, women, and children around the world who are in desperate need of salvation, and it is through Jesus that this can be done. They have so many questions and they need answers right away. This is why sharing the gospel is important. But it is through receiving the anointing, that this desire can (and will) be fulfilled. There is a longing in God's heart that His lost creation be restored back to Him through the acceptance of His Son; as people hear about the gospel, they will learn about the love of God, the perfect gift He sent to the world (His Son), and why the sacrifice of Jesus was needed to cover our sins.

Seek God for more of the Holy Spirit. Just to reiterate, the moment a person gives their life to Jesus, they have just received the anointing through the Holy Spirit. However, you can still go before the Father in prayer and ask Him for more of His anointing through the Holy Spirit. In Matthew 7:7-8 (NIV), Jesus said:

> *"Ask and it will be given to you; seek and you will find; knock and the door will be opened to you. For everyone who asks receives; the one who seeks finds; and to the one who knocks, the door will be opened."*

You would never be asking for too much if you ask God for more of His Spirit - the Holy Spirit. Pray to Him as often as you need to so that you can receive the fullness of the anointing that the Father has for you.

Again, it is important to understand that Christians are anointed to do God's work, but just because you are anointed, that doesn't mean that you should be prideful about it. There have been so many people who started off humble in their anointing but as time went on, they began to allow themselves to be puffed up in their own minds to believe that they are doing great things instead of giving God the glory for doing great things through them for His glory. This is a dangerous place to be in because as Proverbs 16:18 (NIV) says, *"Pride goes before destruction, a haughty [arrogant] spirit before a fall."*

The Benefits of Having God's Anointing

- You will be protected
- Yokes and bondages will be broken
- Your discernment will be sharpened
- Lost blessings in your life will be restored
- You will be connected to God-fearing, like-minded people
- The words you prophetically speak will come to pass
- The reverence and honor you have for God will increase
- You will become more motivated to do even greater things for God
- God will place it in the hearts of others to show/give you favor
- You will be above and not beneath
- You will be able to move at a faster rate spiritually
- You will become a new person
- You will become more impactful for God
- No matter who comes against you or what comes your way, you will be able to conquer every obstacle

How Do You Reach for a Higher Anointing?

Spending a lot time in prayer and fasting is how you will be able to grow in the anointing of God. If your faith is reflecting what you are seeking the Father for and there's no wavering in you, the anointing will be able to flow that much easier through you.

If you are not pleased with where you are in God, that is a strong indicator that there needs to be more intimacy and a deeper commitment in your relationship with the Father. Being comfortable with where you are in God will not get you to the higher levels you need to reach in Him. Going through the routine of just checking the boxes on your "Christian list" will not activate more of an anointing in your life. It takes you having a desire to want it and a willingness to go after it. How much are you willing to give up to go up?

As you press more into God and go deeper with the opportunities you receive from Him, He will increase your growth in the anointing; as a result of that, you will be able live a life that is anointed for the purpose of impacting more people than you will ever know. Get your attention off yourself and start directing your focus to a higher level of thinking; as you do, you will find yourself growing more and more in the anointing of God.

---

1. Anoint. (n.d.). Retrieved January 23, 2018, from http://www.dictionary.com/browse/anoint?s=t

6

DRAWING CLOSER TO GOD'S HEART

"Draw near to God, and he will draw near to you..."

— JAMES 4:8 (ESV)

To draw near to God means to come closer to Him. This is not something that is required without a promise being connected to it. When we take the initiative to move closer to God, He will do His part by moving closer to us. By doing this, the Father is showing an amazing amount of mercy towards us. He does not have to give anything to us, but He chooses to withhold nothing from us- how awesome is that! This is His reply to us as we decide to draw closer to Him.

Wait, God has a Heart?

People have a desire to be known, but what it really comes down to is a longing to be understood by those we deeply love. The reason for this is because we were created in the image of God. He yearns for us to get to know Him and establish a relationship with Him.

If you want to get to know a person, it takes more than just knowing what you see on the surface of that individual. When it comes to God, the same thing applies. It takes more than just knowing of Him, He wants us to get to know Him. The Father wants us close to Him so that we can know how He's doing, how He feels, and what His purposes and plans are for us. Please understand that we'll never know everything about God, but we can get a better understanding of His heart by wanting to know who He is. The Father wants you in the closeness of His heart so that He can pour the love that is in Him on you. He wants you closer to Him more than what you realize but in order for this to happen, you have to allow yourself to draw closer to Him.

Proof of God's Heart Through the Love He Shows

So many people do not know that God has a heart. This goes back to the love- the unconditional love - that the Father has for all of us. Below are a few Scriptures that talk about and/or describe the love God has for His creation:

> "For God so loved the world that he gave his one and only Son, that whoever believes in him shall not perish but have eternal life."

— JOHN 3:16 (NIV)

The Father has so much love for us that He had His Son Jesus come to this earth and die on a cross. The reason why He allowed this to happen is because all of us are sinners and the end result of sin is death (being separated from God for eternity). No matter how good we think we are, we will never be able to make it to heaven based on our good works so God provided a way for us. Jesus Christ is perfect - there is no sin found in Him, and because of that, He allowed Himself to be a sacrifice for our sins. He openly and willingly took our place on the cross because that's how much He loves us. It's only by God's grace and mercy, believing that Jesus died for our sins, and asking Him to forgive our sins, that we can live with Him for eternity in heaven.

"But God demonstrates his own love for us in this: While we were still sinners, Christ died for us."

— ROMANS 5:8 (NIV)

God's love operates on a much higher level than we will ever understand. God offering up His Son as a sacrifice and allowing Him to die represented His love for us. No requirements must be completed in order to receive the love that God already has for us. He makes His love available to all of us; He loves us before we decide to come to Him.

God doesn't love the way we love. We conditionally love people. We love people based on what they can do for us, if they make us happy, what they give us, or what we can get from them. But as soon as they do something to us that we don't like or we get tired of being with/around them, we don't love them anymore. God, on the other hand, loves us unconditionally. He doesn't care who you are, what color you are, where you have come from, what political party you prefer to support, your social status, or anything in between because He sees us all the same - as His creation. God even loves us when we don't love Him, and He proved that when He allowed Jesus to die for us.

"But you, O Lord, are a compassionate and gracious God, slow to anger, abounding in love and faithfulness."

— *PSALM 86:15 (NIV)*

The words *grace* and *mercy* are so commonly used that the meaning of them may not fully be understood. In defining it as simple as possible, mercy is when God withholds the worst that we deserve but chooses to show forgiveness and compassion instead. Grace is when we do not deserve God's best (unmerited favor, blessings, etc.) but He allows us to receive it. God is so gracious towards us that He gives us so many chances while we are living this life. It is through His mercy that we are able to benefit from His grace and favor that is pleasing and enjoyable for us.

"Though the mountains be shaken and the hills be removed, yet my unfailing love for you will not be shaken nor my covenant of peace be removed,' says the Lord, who has compassion on you."

— *ISAIAH 54:10 (NIV)*

In this Scripture, God uses the illustration of mountains and hills to express the importance of His covenant. When you look at them, mountains and hills appear to be stable. But as introducing mountains being removed and hills shaking, the Father is saying that nothing is more secure than the covenant He has with and for His people. Even if the mountains are removed, the covenant of His love and loyalty will stay. Even if the hills shake, God's peace will still be there. The love that God has for us is unshakeable and unmovable. No matter what the situations or circumstances are, God gives us His promise that His love and peace will never be taken away from us.

How Do You Draw Closer to God's Heart?

Desiring to draw closer to God's heart is not only a great goal to reach for, it also reveals the heart of those who are deeply in Jesus who want to establish a stronger relationship with Him. No matter where you are in your walk with Christ or how long you have been walking with Christ, there's always room for you to draw closer to Him. Here are a few things that you can do to start drawing closer to God's heart:

Confess Your Sins to God

Confessing our sins daily to God is a must. If the reason you are not able to draw closer to God's heart is because of sin, that obstacle has to be removed so that you will be able to connect more with Him. God will forgive our sins when we confess them to Him and when we do, we are able to reestablish our relationship with Him that had become strained due to our sins. Let me also add that it takes more than just saying, "I'm sorry I sinned against you, God," and then you go on your way. When you confess your sins to God, it will cause a change in your heart to take place because you realize that sin breaks the heart of the Father; this is what true repentance looks like. It is also through your confession that you realize that your sins are the reason why Jesus was crucified so that you can become more aware of how critical your sins are.

Read God's Word

God reveals the character of Himself through His Word. The Bible will reveal who God is, what He has done (what He is doing and going to do), and what it is He expects of us as His creation. But even as powerful and holy as the Father is, He still wants us to approach Him so that we can draw closer to Him; reading His Word will allow that door to open. God longs for us to be close to Him to the point that He comes looking for us so that He can establish a relationship with us. Even though we are sinners, He still wants the intimacy of having His creation close to Him, and the way to receive that is through His Word. It is through the Father's Word that He seeks the lost and shows us the sacrifice He made for us through His Son Jesus so that we can be restored back to Him as well as be ambassadors for the glory of His Kingdom.

Pray to God

As I stated earlier, prayer is a two-way conversation between you and God. It opens the door for you to nurture a more solid relationship with Him by talking to Him and allowing Him to talk to you. Even Jesus went away in secret to pray to the Father often; so, if He did it, it should be a part of our relationship-building process with the Father as well. Although you can come to God in prayer about anything, it is more than just coming to Him when you only want or need something from Him. It's you choosing to come to Him simply because of who He is and you wanting to get to know Him for who He is, and as you grow more in the inward parts of prayer, you will grow more in the inward parts of God and His heart.

Listen to God's Voice

God speaks to all of us, but we choose whether or not to accept what He is saying and be properly positioned to hear His voice. It is in the stillness of silence that you can hear God's voice. You have to learn how to humble yourself before Him and let His words guide you along the process. Allow His words to live inside of you and breathe life in you. In other words, prepare yourself more by hearing God speak. So how do you hear the Father speak? By being still and knowing that He is God (Psalm 46:10).

God speaks to those who are quiet - not the ones whose minds are not cluttered with the things of this world but the ones who are focused on Him. Their thoughts and hearts are attentive to Him and what He has for them. The enemy will try to distract you when you want to hear from God. He will do so by putting worries or thoughts of unconcern in your mind. Or if you are focused on God, the enemy will distract you by making the telephone ring, enticing you to go over your to-do list for the day, and so many other ways. Rest in the stillness of the Father's presence and allow yourself to hear from Him, and as you do, you will find yourself drawing closer to Him.

Walk in the Obedience of God

For some, obeying God can be difficult. This difficulty can increase even more when we convince ourselves to believe that we are going to miss out on so much more if we obey than we would if we choose to do the opposite. This is false because obedience is important if you want to draw closer to God. We accept a standard from the Father when we allow ourselves to obey Him.

So many positive results come from obeying God. We operate in His wisdom as we choose to obey Him. The more we obey God, the more He is able to teach us about Himself, His love, and His principles. Getting to know the Father more becomes easier as we continue to obey Him because we will be more receptive to receiving obedience as opposed to feeling that it is being forced on us. This is because God knows the consequences that we could suffer if we disobey Him, so He loves us enough to offer His heart as a way to avoid that.

7

WHEN DOUBT EMERGES

"But when you ask, you must believe and not doubt, because the one who doubts is like a wave of the sea, blown and tossed by the wind. That person should not expect to receive anything from the Lord. Such a person is double-minded and unstable in all they do."

— JAMES 1:6-8 (NIV)

D oubt emerges within us when we encounter or face something that doesn't equal what we identify with God. Doubt should not be confused with the absence of a promise. When we have doubts, it's not a matter as to whether we think God loves us or if our faith in God is real, but it's about God Himself - if He really is with us or if His nature is genuine.

A biblical example of doubt would be Job. Job was an honorable and devoted man whose primary focus was to walk in the ways of God. He was faithful to God and served Him with a true heart. However, devastation paid Job a visit. He lost all of his children, part of his livestock was stolen (and the other part was slaughtered), the majority of his servants were killed, and his whole body was afflicted with painful boils. All of the mishaps and circumstances that Job had faced was no fault of his own. Job knew that God was excellent and holy, but what he was going through didn't match what he was facing; because of that, doubt came in.

Why Does Doubt Happen?

We have to understand that we won't know everything and because of that, we can't see the overall picture of what is in front of us. When we are not able to comprehend what is before us, it could cause us to doubt. We have to be mindful of the fact that the Father created us with limitations. Everything wasn't meant for us to figure out because if it was, there would not be any room in our lives to trust and rely on God.

The voice of the enemy (which I will discuss later in this chapter) will cause us to doubt God and what He says. If we allow the enemy to convince us to doubt God and then we do what the enemy is making to appear "better" than what God is saying, we have just allowed room for sin to take place in our life.

How Do We Deal with Doubt?

Doubt is something that we all have experienced, but how do we handle it? If we are not personally dealing with doubt, how do we support those around us who are operating in it?

Do not be alarmed by the doubt you see. For some, getting over doubt is not as easy as it seems. If someone comes to you wanting to discuss their doubt issues, be respectful enough to hear what they have to say. You may not have the answers and you may not be able to relate to what they are saying, but being willing to listen shows that you have a sense of concern for the person and their issue. Take whatever they tell you seriously, offer to pray for them, and give them reference to God's Word for strength and encouragement so that their faith can increase.

Do not allow doubt to isolate you. During those moments when you feel doubt emerging, find someone to talk to, preferably someone you feel that you can trust. For some, talking about doubt in the church can be seen as taboo, but when you are able to open up to someone that you trust, it lifts the burden and it will make you feel more at ease about this issue. If the person you chose to confide in refuses to hear what you have to say, go to someone who will but do not hold those doubtful concerns inside of you. Or better yet, let God know how you feel about the doubt that's trying to emerge and operate through you.

Do not be prideful. Although we shouldn't be alarmed when doubt emerges, we shouldn't allow ourselves to become prideful about it either. We have to humble ourselves and find help in reading God's Word because the solution to the problem of doubt can be found in Scripture. In order for doubt to be conquered, it takes one being willing to move in humility.

Do not lose sight of the big picture. When we look through the lens of doubt, we see what we are viewing and experiencing at that particular moment. We only see a fraction of the full picture and at times, our view can be misleading. During these times, it's important to know that your "right now" moment is not forever. The Father already knows what you are going through and He knows how you feel. However, redirecting your focus on Him would be of great benefit. Realizing that God knows us is more important than anything else. Dwelling in doubt can make you feel like you are in a dark place, but when you allow the love of Jesus to shine through you, it will quickly burn out the doubt that's trying to hold on to you.

Who is Satan?

Satan is a liar. John 8:44 (NLT) says, *"He was a murderer from the beginning and has always hated the truth. There is no truth in him. When he lies he is consistent with his character; for he is a liar and the father of lies."* The reason why Satan is good at lying is because his lies sound extremely close to the truth. He does this to alter your way of thinking so that he will be able to trick and defeat you. Not only is the enemy known as being the father of lies, but his main topic of preference to lie about is God.

If Satan can successfully manage to twist your thinking about God and have you believe that his lies about the Father are true, he has just grabbed hold of you and every area of your life. Satan is now ruler over you when you allow him to plant his deceitful seeds in your mind.

Satan uses his power to control. First John 5:19 (WEB) says, *"We know that we are of God, and the whole world lies in the power of the evil one."* Even though Satan has powers, the powers he has are limited to what God allows him to have and what He allows him to do; because of this, we have no reason to be afraid of the enemy, his demons, and what they do or try to do to us. On the other hand, it's important not to forget that even with limitations, Satan still has powers because he controls the things of this world, but not forever. The day will come when Satan will be punished for the evil he has done and is doing to God's creation but until that day, he will continue to find ways to deceive, suppress, confuse, entice, destroy, and control us, even if it means using others to do it.

Satan is a destroyer. In the first part of John 10:10 (NIV), it says, *"The thief comes only to steal and kill and destroy."* The thoughts the enemy and evil spirits plant in your mind are done for three reasons:

1. To steal from you (your mind, blessings, calling, breakthroughs, etc.)
2. To kill you (whether it be spiritually or physically)
3. To destroy you (your name, character, reputation, God's plan for your life, etc.)

Although Satan will never be able to take us to the point where the Father isn't able to reach us, he will try everything he can to paralyze and spiritually destroy us so that we will not be of any use for the work of Christ. One of many things that gives the enemy satisfaction is when we are in a confused state and question who we are in God and what He is calling us to do.

Satan is one who deceives. Revelation 12:9 (ESV) says, *"And the great dragon was thrown down, that ancient serpent, who is* *called the devil and Satan, the deceiver of the whole world—he was thrown down to the earth, and his angels were thrown down with him."* Satan's primary goal is to deceive us. The enjoyment he gets from deceiving people is when they have no idea that he is deceiving them. There will be times when it will be hard to determine if the enemy is trying to deceive us and if we are able to see through his deception (through discernment and the leading of the Holy Spirit), he's going to leave and return when he finds a different way to carry out his deceptive plan against us. This is why keeping yourself secured and anchored in God is important.

The Voice of the Enemy

When engaging in spiritual warfare, it's important to know when we hear Satan's voice. When I say Satan's voice, I'm not talking about a voice that we hear audibly. I'm speaking in regards to the thoughts that are planted in our minds by him. The enemy's voice is inserted in the same area where we form our own thoughts.

God wants us to recognize the voice of the enemy. Satan has no problem with speaking, which is why it's important to be aware of everything the enemy is saying to us. Throughout the Bible, Satan speaks in different ways. He spoke as a serpent in the Garden of Eden when he gave Eve deceitful information about the tree of knowledge of good and evil, and by getting to her, he was able to get to Adam (Genesis 3:1-6). He spoke through Goliath and caused the Israelites to be afraid of him (1 Samuel 17:8-11; 42-44). He spoke through the spirits (called Legion) that possessed the man who lived in the tombs (Mark 5:2-9). There are so many examples I could use to prove this, but the bottom line is that the enemy knows how to talk and if we are not careful, we will listen to him.

What Happens When You Listen to the Voice of the Enemy?

- Fear will overtake you
- You will become doubtful
- You will develop a sense of discomfort
- You will be robbed of your peace
- You will dwell in a place of restlessness
- You will live in a confused state
- You will become condemned (full of guilt and shame)
- You will become discouraged
- You could end up denying Jesus Christ
- You could end up turning your back on God

Strategies to Silence the Voice of the Enemy

Know God's Word. Recognizing God's voice through His Word is needed to shut down the enemy's voice. When we know what the Father says in His Word, we will know that what the enemy tries to speak to us doesn't line up with what God has already said about us. When we understand that God's Word is bigger than the enemy, we no longer have to take heed to the words the enemy is speaking to us. This is what will stop us from falling prey to the schemes of the enemy and allowing ourselves to be open for him to defeat us.

Relying on God's Word takes faith but in doing so, you will be able to defeat the enemy by using the Father's Word against him. When you find a Scripture that pertains to your situations or circumstances and you use it against the enemy, you've just destroyed him and the work he had set up against you. The next time you hear the voice of the enemy, do not allow yourself to absorb what he is saying. Do what Jesus did in the wilderness and speak the Word of God against him (Matthew 4:1-11; Luke 4:1-13). Every time Jesus spoke the Word, He shut the enemy down. And guess what? You have the power to do the same thing thanks to the example Christ set for us and His power and authority that lives in us.

Test the thoughts you hear. When thoughts come into your mind, you can check to see if they are coming from God or if they are coming from Satan. By doing this, you will then know where you need to go with making your decisions. For instance, thoughts could come into your mind such as, "God doesn't hear your prayers. God doesn't love you. Just give up, you're not getting anywhere." If you are not careful, you will find yourself entertaining these thoughts because the enemy has twisted your thinking. But before you allow this to happen, do something about the thoughts you are hearing by rebuking them, and replacing these lies with the Father's truth. If you fail to do this, you are leaving yourself open for the enemy to attack you.

Receive God's forgiveness and let Him renew your mind. God wants to rebuke the enemy for your sake, and no matter what the enemy tells you, your sins were forgiven when Jesus was sacrificed on the cross. So, if the enemy tries to bring up your sins, let him know that they have been washed away by the Savior's blood.

Allow the Father to heal your mind from what the enemy tried to do to it. Let Him renew your mind so that you can remember who you are to Him, how important you are to Him, and how you are seen through His eyes.

Take faith steps. When you step out on faith - to go against the enemy - you are increasing your authority. Have faith in knowing that the Father is guiding you and He will give you everything you need to destroy the enemy for His glory. You are not in this battle alone. God is with you and He is fighting for you! So, when Satan tries to attack your mind with fear, untrue thoughts, false accusations, hurt, doubt, or unbelief, surrender those thoughts to God and let Him fight your battles and destroy the enemy for you.

8

OBEYING GOD'S WORD

"If you are willing and obedient, you will eat the good things of the land."

— ISAIAH 1:19 (NIV)

The Benefits of Being Obedient to God's Word

The benefits of being obedient to God's Word (in regards to reading, studying, meditating, and reflecting on the Bible) are more than we could ever be able to count. Although so much is covered in the Bible, there can be times when we have a tendency to gravitate towards certain Scriptures more than others. We learn a lot in the Bible about the Father, what He has laid out for us, and His will and desires for us. Through God's Word, you can receive assurance, support, and peace. We also have been able to experience guidance and direction on a daily basis. These are just a few things that we can receive from being obedient to God's Word but as we go further into His Word, we will be able to receive more of what He has for us. Below are more benefits listed as a result of being obedient to God's Word:

We will be prepared for what is to come. It is through God's Word that He is able to develop our patience and give us the encouragement that we need for whatever lies ahead of us. During those moments in our lives when we are going through pain, persecution, or circumstances, it is through God's Word that we will be able to stand because it is His Word that prepares the way to lead us to victory.

You will be able to resist the traps of the enemy. When Jesus had finished fasting for 40 days, the enemy came to Him three times to tempt Him; every time the enemy came at Jesus with some form of temptation, He was able to defeat the enemy with Scripture. It is God's Word that will keep us from sinning because God's Word is the truth that covers and protects us from the harmful attacks of the enemy, which results in us acting in obedience towards Him.

You will grow spiritually. It is in the heart of the Father that we desire to become more like His Son Jesus; so as we obey God's Word, it boosts our spiritual maturity and causes us to grow more in Him. Obeying God's Word will change our mindset from what we want to what God needs. It will also shape us into the likeness of Christ and nurture our spirit. Becoming more receptive to spiritual growth will cause us to become more knowledgeable in the things of Christ so that we can grow and become rooted in our relationship with Him.

A level of increase will take place in your life. As you continue to remain obedient to God's Word, your life will flourish. This will happen because God will bless you for committing yourself to His Word and what it requires of you to do. It will create everlasting results that will go beyond natural thinking while pulling you closer to Him at the same time.

Answers to Prayers: The Story of Hannah

When it comes to going before God in prayer, we have to make sure that we come with the right heart and continue to go before Him in the right manner. If you feel that there is sin present in your life, make sure that you repent so that God will forgive you and there will be no room for you to condemn yourself. First John 3:22 (NLT) says, *"And we will receive from him whatever we ask because we obey him and do the things that please him."* When it comes to our prayers being answered, this Scripture can be broken down in two ways:

1. **When we obey what God says, He will answer our prayers.** As your heart becomes more filled up with God's Word, you will allow more room to receive the Father's values, facts, and instructions, and the easier it will become for you to obey Him. As you obey God, the door will open so that your prayers can be answered by Him.

2. **When we do what pleases God, He will answer our prayers.** It is important to know that you have to do what pleases God, not yourself. You should teach your heart to be more like Jesus'. He proudly proclaimed that He was, "about His Father's business" (Luke 2:49). He had no problem making it

known that He did everything to please the Father (John 8:29), and we should be the same way. All that should be done is so that God will be pleased with us.

Take Hannah for example. In 1 Samuel 1:1-20, there is an Ephraimite named Elkanah. Elkanah had two wives named Peninnah and Hannah. Peninnah had several children but Hannah did not have any. Every year, Elkanah would take his family to Shiloh to offer sacrifices to God. Elkanah would give Peninnah and their children a portion of meat, but Hannah would receive a double portion because Elkanah loved her more than he loved Peninnah; because of this, Peninnah became jealous of Hannah.

She would taunt Hannah as an attempt to make her feel bad about herself because she was childless. Year after year, Peninnah would do this to Hannah until she became angry and irritated by Peninnah's immature tactics. Hannah was grieved in her soul so she desperately cried out and prayed to the Lord. Hannah promised God that if He blessed her with a son, she would dedicate her child back to Him and never shave his head.

Shortly after Elkanah and Hannah returned home, she became pregnant. She had a son and named him Samuel, whose name means "Because I asked the Lord for him." Hannah inclined - or delighted herself - in God. Hannah had a need. She released her bitterness, brokenness, and emptiness over to God and as a result of that, He granted Hannah what she requested: a son who would later grow up to become a well-known prophet in Israel.

No Curses

Where do curses come from? In the Bible, you will read where blessings and curses are discussed in Deuteronomy 28:15-68. Blessings manifest when you obey God, but curses take place when you disobey Him. Curses happen when someone does something that goes against God's Word. Whatever act was committed that goes against Scripture will not only bring a curse on you, but to your children and future generations after you. From here on out, the enemy's job is to make sure that this curse stays in place and affects all generations that come after you. Scripture tells us in Numbers 14:18 (ESV) that curses come to us because of the sins that our fathers (ancestors) have committed:

> *"The LORD is slow to anger and abounding in steadfast love, forgiving iniquity and transgression, but he will by no means clear the guilty, visiting the iniquity of the fathers on the children, to the third and the fourth generation."*

Because of the curse that happened in Genesis 3, Satan now had power to destroy the Father's creation and with this power came a release of the enemy's demons all over the world.

Receiving Blessings: The Story of Abraham and Isaac

There are so many people who received blessings from God because they chose to obey Him. One of the people who falls under this category is Abraham. He is known as the father of many nations, but he did not start off that way. This obedience walk began for Abram (his original name that was changed to Abraham when God established a covenant with him) in Genesis 12 when God told him to leave his country and go to the land He would lead him to, which would later end up being Canaan. Abraham took his wife Sarai (who would later become Sarah) and left without hesitation. By the time Abraham left Haran, he was already 75 years old but even in his old age, God promised that he would make him a great nation and make his name great (Genesis 12:2).

Abraham believed in the covenant God made with him and years later, Sarah became pregnant - when she was 90 years old and Abraham was 100 years old - and gave birth to a son named Isaac. It is through Isaac that the promise to Abraham was carried out. Through Isaac, the whole earth would be blessed because through Abraham's descendants, the Savior came into the world. Jesus was the fulfillment of the promise that was made.

God spoke to Abraham when he was 75 years old, but his promised child wasn't born until he was 100 years old. That's 25 years Abraham held on to a word that God gave him before he saw it come to pass.

In Genesis 21, Isaac was born but as you read the next chapter, we now see that God is testing Abraham in regards to Isaac. As Abraham's faith grew, God instructed him to give his son Isaac as a sacrifice to prove how faithful Abraham was to Him. Abraham obeyed God and took Isaac to Mount Moriah, laid him on an altar he had built and just moments before Abraham was about to sacrifice his son, God told him not to kill him. Instead, the Father told him to sacrifice a ram that was in a bush nearby. Again, Abraham remembered the promise God told him about Isaac. He had enough faith and obedience to believe that God would not have sent him a son just to have him sacrificed because it was through Isaac that Abraham was going to have an innumerable amount of descendants throughout the earth.

Abraham taught us a valuable lesson: as long as you continue to obey the words that God speaks to you, you will continue to receive the blessings that He has for you. Do not look at your situations, or even yourself, as a measure to determine if God will fulfill the promises He has for you. Walk in the obedience of His Word believing that He has already fulfilled His blessings for you. Keep believing that what God speaks to you is what He has already done for you.

9

THE DISTORTED IMAGE OF SELF-ESTEEM

Self-esteem is used to describe a person's overall sense of self-worth or personal value. In other words, how much you appreciate and like yourself. Self-esteem is often seen as a personality trait, which means that it tends to be stable and enduring. Self-esteem can involve a variety of beliefs about yourself such as the appraisal of your own appearance, beliefs, emotions, and behaviors.[1]

How Is Self-Esteem Distorted?

Rejection. Everybody has either been rejected in some shape or form, or they are going through rejection right now. It is one of the most common forms of spiritual oppression that must be dealt with immediately in order for people to be released and set free. It causes more damage than most people realize, and it's not noticed until it's too late. It's important to know how it operates and what you can do to stop it from going any further.

Why Does Rejection Hurt So Bad?

Rejection is launched out with the intent to do harm to us. It tears down our self-esteem and destroys us as well as the calling and destiny that God has for us. Rejection is a regular tactic that the enemy uses to cause devastation in our life. It was never a part of God's plan that we experience rejection. He not only wants you to know how much He loves you. He also wants you to know your identity so that you can carry out the purpose that He has sent you to this earth to fulfill.

Rejection can ruin someone's life to the point where they feel that there's no way they will ever be able to heal from it. The amount of people who have experienced rejection (especially amongst believers) is disappointing. In order to live out this life doing what God has called us to do, we have to understand the importance of being healed and delivered from rejection.

When Does Rejection Begin?

Rejection begins the moment we lose ourselves. In other words, it starts the moment we lose the identity of who we are. Anytime we allow ourselves to be shaped and formed by certain things (social status, jobs, ministries, businesses, etc.,) or start paying attention to what people have to say about us instead of believing what God says about us in His Word, we've just allowed ourselves to become exposed to rejection.

The opinions and actions of other people (parents, family members, friends, associates, teachers, employers, co-workers, church members, etc.,) can greatly contribute to causing us to lose focus of who we are, Who created us, and what we were created for. This commonly starts in the earlier stages of life, which is serious because the identities of children are being formed. This can also carry on through the teenage years where it becomes worst because of the pressure they feel to fit in but end up being rejected because they don't fit a certain "image" whether they feel they are too tall, too short, too big, too thin, too quiet, too loud, too light, too dark, not wearing the most expensive clothes/shoes, the social status of their family, or whatever the case may be. This is usually initiated by children who don't know who they are, so they try to destroy who others as an attempt to feel good about themselves.

The Outward Result of Rejection

The more rejection is invoked on a child while they are growing up, the more emotional damage it causes. If this emotional damage is not resolved, it will cause spiritual damage that will go even deeper. This spiritual damage can go deep and result in low self-esteem, jealously, envy, and unforgiveness, or you may even get to the point of blaming and questioning God. Once the spiritual damage has been done, the enemy can now seize the moment to keep us bound by replaying and reliving scenarios in our minds that happened years ago, or we may allow resentment and negative thoughts to remain inside of us that are directed towards other people, God, and even ourselves.

The effects of rejection can easily transfer to us or those who are around us. A few of the warning signs that you should be on the lookout for in regards to rejection are:

- You feel that you don't fit in or you are not received by others.
- Jealously, envy, and/or hatred is either directed towards you or you are directing it towards others.
- Being afraid of what others will think or say about you.
- You are a perfectionist (afraid of failing).
- You feel that you are in a helpless and hopeless state.
- You or someone else feels sorry about being alone.
- You feel the need to be right about everything.
- Rebellion is present in children and adults.
- You refuse to be corrected or accept the opinions of those who are trying to help you.
- The thought always crosses your mind whether people will stay in your life or walk out of it.
- Always needing acceptance from other people.
- You reject people first (whether there's a reason to or not) to avoid being rejected.
- Self-rejection (when a person dislikes or hates something about themselves or they are not willing to forgive themselves).
- You want to be and feel loved by others.

Lies and Slander

Satan is known as the father of lies (John 8:44) and the accuser of brethren (Revelation 12:10). So why does he lie? The reason is because he wants to destroy us and if he's able to succeed, it will stop us from carrying out the assignment (calling) that God has for us to do. The lies that the enemy tries to release can come to us from different directions.

They can come from those we know or know of (friends, family members, spouses, girlfriend/boyfriend, church members, etc.,), or they can come from what is being portrayed in the media that we allow to get our attention.

It's imperative that we keep this in mind because not only will the enemy have lies launched directly at us, but there may be someone who comes to you that has been lied to or lied about, which has caused them to be entangled by traps of the enemy. This is why it is important to know God's Word and walk in discernment so that we can recognize the lies the enemy tries to present.

Also, when it comes to the body of Christ (believers), the enemy will do everything in his power to stop God's work from going forth by releasing lies and slander. The ones who are willing to listen to him are the ones he can convince. He's even bold enough at times to slander us by getting in our minds and spiritually poisoning us (condemnation) if we aren't anchored in God.

Being Reminded of Your Past

The enemy uses other people to bring up our past. I've had those moments where I went years without being in contact with people I was either friends with or just acquaintances. Initially (for the people I was familiar with the most), I would actually look forward to it. You get to catch up and see what's currently going on in the life of this person. But sometimes, within moments of reuniting, my feelings would shift from being excited to see this person to being excited that the encounter is over. The reason is because the majority of the time, the person was interested in talking about my past and who I used to be rather than being interested in the person I have now become since they saw me X amount of years ago.

I've had people who would remind me of the things that I used to do and the things I used to say. Sometimes when this happened, I'd politely respond by letting the person know that I don't remember doing or saying what they are talking about, which usually results in them giving me a photographic description (almost to the point of where they're getting upset) to try to make me remember what I said/did. After they're finished with this flashback, I respond by either saying, "Although I don't remember doing/saying this, it sounds like something I could've said/done, but that's not who I am today," or "Yeah, I do remember saying/doing that, but I'm not that person anymore; I left that behind me."

I then try to redirect the conversation and introduce them to the person they are communicating with now as an attempt for them to get to know the "new me," but the conversation usually goes backwards instead of moving forward. They insist on going back to the past so it doesn't matter where I am today; in their minds, I'm still where I was doing what I was doing X amount of years ago. When this happens, I usually cut the conversation short and then cut the person off.

My past isn't one of the cleanest. I've done things that I'm not proud of. I've said things that caused more harm than help. I wasn't as attentive to my actions back then as I am now. I travelled some roads that caused some serious, life-changing detours in my life. I was an adult when I rededicated my life back to Christ; prior to me getting saved, I didn't have a care or a conscience about some of the things I said/did. But there's something about being able to find refuge in God's Word, isn't it? It always brings me joy!

Second Corinthians 5:17 (KJV) says, *"Therefore if any man be in Christ, he is a **new** creature: **old** things are passed away; behold, **all** things are become new."* The moment we accept Jesus into our life, our sins are covered and washed away by His blood that was shed and used as an atonement for our sins. There's no recollection of the things that we did/didn't do. How do I know this? Because Micah 7:19 (NIV) says, *"You [God] will again have compassion on us; you will tread our sins underfoot and hurl all our iniquities into the depths of the sea."* Another translation that is used for this Scripture is that God casts our sins into the sea of forgetfulness. So, if this is the case, why are we still coming across people who feel the need to bring up our past?

Some people will bring up your past without the intent of a hidden agenda behind it. They like reminiscing about the "good old days" or the good times of the past. These are the moments where you both can laugh and find enjoyment about it. However, there are others who are fully aware of what they are doing but choose to push the envelope anyway. These are the people who are allowing themselves to be used by the enemy. They will use this as an opportunity to steer the conversation in the direction they want it to go for the remainder of this encounter, which is manipulation. It makes them feel as if they have something to hold over you.

Believe it or not, these are the moments that you need to face in order to know whether or not you've actually dealt with your past. If you've asked God to forgive your past and you have turned from who you were and the things you used to do, it will be very easy for you to disregard what others are saying and walk away from it. However, if what they're saying is causing you to become ashamed, nervous, or offensive, not only does it mean that you haven't dealt with your past, it also means that you don't have the faith to believe that Jesus covered your sins with His blood. This is what the enemy is aiming for. He wants you to remain imprisoned by a past that Jesus has already set you free from.

The enemy uses us to bring up our own past. One of the most common tactics the enemy tries to use against us is a device called guilt. This is why so many believers are living their lives feeling crushed and overwhelmed. Guilt makes them feel defeated, steals their confidence, places them in a pitiful state, and causes a feeling of separation from Christ. Jesus wanted to do more than just wash us clean of the sins we carried, He also wanted to get rid of the weight of guilt that came as a result of our sins.

The enemy gets pure enjoyment out of causing us to suffer when he reminds us of our past, and he constantly dangles our sins over our heads. This even happens after we know that the sins we committed have already been forgiven by the Father. This is called condemnation, and the final consequence of it is not good. It will leave you feeling weak, hopeless, and deprived of the assurance that God has given you.

The guilt of your past is able to manifest when you are in constant thought about your past and all of things you did or didn't do. Whenever you do this, it brings the enemy satisfaction because he's now able to keep your mind suppressed with these negative thoughts. This is why Apostle Paul said in Philippians 4:8 (ESV), *"Finally, brothers, whatever is true, whatever is honorable, whatever is just, whatever is pure, whatever is lovely, whatever is commendable, if there is any excellence, if there is anything worthy of praise, **think about these things**."* If we choose to think about our past instead of reflecting on the goodness of God, we will cause our minds to become weakened to the truth and the love that He has for us.

As the enemy further opens the door of guilt, it allows room for other unwanted things to enter inside of us such as not being able to forgive ourselves. When the enemy is able to convince you that you shouldn't forgive yourself, you are causing a further division to come between you and the love the Father wants to give to you. You will not be able to receive the pureness of God's heart because of a harmful misconception brought on by the enemy himself. This false belief could cause further damage by building up bitterness in your heart towards God to the point where you don't want anything to do with Him; this is exactly where the enemy wants you: completely out of the will of God.

---

1. Cherry, K. (n.d.). Find out Why Self-Esteem Is Important for Success. Retrieved January 23, 2018, from https://www.verywell.com/what-is-self-esteem-2795868

10

RESIST TAKING THE BAIT

"But each person is tempted when he is lured and enticed by his own desire."

— JAMES 1:14 (ESV)

When hunters want to catch animals, they use traps that either they have made or they purchase premade traps. Depending on the type of animal a hunter wants to catch, they may use certain foods or plants (also known as bait) to lure the animals into the traps quicker. Other ways hunters create traps to catch animals is to either find or dig a hole in the ground and cover it with something that was in the environment that the animals lived in so that they would not be able to realize that a trap has been set for them. I never went hunting for animals before, but the same tactics hunters use to catch animals were the same tactics I used when I used to fish.

I remember the first time I went fishing with my mom and a few other family members when I was a little girl. My mom had this big fishing pole that she gave to me when we got to the pond. Before she started fishing, she pulled out a small container that had dark soil and a bunch of worms in it. She took out one of the worms, grabbed the fishing hook that was on the end of my pole and quickly pulled and tangled this worm on the hook so that it wouldn't go anywhere. She then looked at me and said, "This is what you have to do to catch your fish." She then took me to the part of the pond where she could see the fish coming to the surface of the water (biting) and said, "You have to bring your arm back and throw your fishing line into the water as far as you can. When the bobble starts bouncing up and down in the water, pull your line back in, but you have to do it fast so that you can catch your fish." And then she turned around, walked away, went a few feet behind me, and started fishing with the rest of my family members.

What she said sounded easy but when it was time for me to put it into practice, it wasn't as easy as it looked. I didn't have any problems with casting my line into the water; the problem came when I was trying to pull my line out of the water before the fish got away. After doing this a few times, I got frustrated and made the mistake of looking behind me and seeing all of the fish my mom and everybody else was catching; it made me pout even harder. Then I thought about it. After a few attempts, it finally hit me: they (the fish) were only biting from sides of the hook because the bait was hanging too far over on the sides of the hook! When the light finally came on in my brain, I got creative with how I began to bait my hook. I was able to bait the worm and pull it higher on the hook with little to any of it hanging over the sides of the hook. I chose to bait the hook this way because I knew that the fish would be so distracted by eating the worm that when they tried to pull away, they would be caught on the hook before they realized what was going on. Now for a small child, this was a lot of work but I didn't mind. I was patient and very attentive to what I was doing because that's how badly I wanted to catch this fish!

After adjusting my strategy, I cast the line into the pond again; shortly after I did, I saw the fishing bobble drop deep in the water, followed by me feeling some resistance at the end of my fishing pole. All of a sudden, I saw a fish flapping in and out of the water. When my mom heard it, she yelled, "Pull, Sherre (my middle name), you got a catch!" It took some work, but I was able to pull this fish in. I was so excited! After watching the fish long enough, I realized that I had to change how I was baiting my fishing hook, and when I did, I was able to hook and pull those fish in every time after that. The more I did it, the easier it became.

When the enemy tries to bait you, he uses traps that are not obvious to see as an effort to hold you hostage and imprison you. So many people (including myself) have traveled down this street but have no knowledge of the traps that have been set up for them. Countless people have taken the bait of the enemy, but just like the fish I caught, by the time they realized it, it was too late. When I realized what I was doing wasn't working with trying to catch that fish, I changed my technique. I changed what I was doing and I was patient so that I could get what I wanted, which were the fish. It's not any different with the enemy. He will place traps, snares, and bait in front of you to see whether or not you will fall for them. He will study and watch you so that he can see what your strengths and weaknesses are so that he will know how to place his bait before you, and he's patient with doing this. Just like with me trying to catch those fish, the enemy will wait however long he has to, use a variety of bait, and do whatever he needs to do to hook and reel you into what he has set up for you.

It's time to be aware of how the enemy is trying to bait us. One of the many ways to do this is to use God's Word as a guide and read the stories about people the enemy used to take his bait and others he tried to use, but they resisted. Whenever we read God's Word, not only are able to use Scripture against the enemy, we can also use these words to block the bait he is trying to use to entice and tempt us with. When we allow ourselves to become submerged in God's Word, we will have a better understanding of how the bait of the enemy works; as a result, we will be able to discern the traps he has set up for us and learn how to stay away from them.

Ways the Enemy Tries to Bait Us

Temptation

When it comes down to it, temptation will come at us in either one of three (or all three) ways: through the lust of the flesh, the lust of the eyes, and the pride of life.[1]

> "For all that is in the world, the lust of the flesh, and the lust of the eyes, and the pride of life, is not of the Father, but is of the world."

In this Scripture, Apostle John identifies the three temptations that exist in the world. It is essential to take note of these temptations that we will encounter them because every sin that we agree to hand ourselves over to originated from one or all three of them:

1. The Lust of the Flesh

The lust of the flesh is a temptation that is carried out as a result of gaining physical pleasure from sinful acts. This sin will take place in a way that brings satisfaction to your flesh (body). Some examples of the lust of the flesh are:

- Backbiting, gossiping, lying, slandering
- Use of alcohol
- Use of drugs (pills, crack, cocaine, marijuana, synthetic marijuana, etc.)
- Violence (physical, assault, etc.)
- Sins involving sex (fornication, adultery, oral sex, anal sex, incest, rape, homosexuality, lesbianism, orgies, masturbation, bestiality, etc.)

2. The Lust of the Eyes

The lust of the eyes is a temptation that involves staring at people or things we shouldn't or desiring to have people or things we're not supposed to have. If you are taking this from a spiritual perspective, it is when we look at people or things in a yearning or satisfying way when God specifically told us not to.

A direct example of this would be a sin that God prohibits in the Bible called coveting. Coveting happens when the lust of the eyes is fulfilled when someone gives into it. Coveting is discussed in the Old Testament as one of the Ten Commandments God gave Moses to tell the Israelites:

"You shall not covet your neighbor's wife."

— DEUTERONOMY 5:21 (NIV)

Wanting another person's spouse is an example of coveting. Being envious of other people and the things and/or people they have is another example. Envy is when you see someone with something that you don't have and you want it for yourself because it appears eye-catching and attractive. This could range from anything like jobs to money and even the way someone looks.

3. The Pride of Life

The pride of life is a temptation that is used to obtain power that we feel we are entitled to. Pride is the sin that took Lucifer from being a beautiful angel in heaven to becoming Satan - our enemy (Ezekiel 28:12-19). A few examples of the pride of life are:

- Craving to receive recognition or praise for what others (or even God) accomplished
- Wanting people to reverence or honor you so that you can use it to promote yourself
- Feeling the need to be exalted so that you will feel more important than the people around you

- Wanting to receive certain positions or titles to become puffed up and boastful because you have authority over other people

It was pride that caused Satan to get kicked out of heaven:

"I [Satan] will ascend above the tops of the clouds; I will make myself like the Most High [God]. "

— ISAIAH 14:14 (NIV)

It was never Satan's desire to overthrow God. Satan wanted to rise above God so that He would have power and control over Him. His planned failed but he didn't stop there. As a result of being kicked out of heaven, Satan decided to get back at God. In Genesis 2:15-17 (NIV), God gave Adam stewardship and specific instructions while he was in the Garden of Eden:

"The Lord God took the man [Adam] and put him in the Garden of Eden to work it and take care of it. And the Lord God commanded the man, "You are free to eat from any tree in the garden; but you must not eat from the tree of the knowledge of good and evil, for when you eat from it you will certainly die."

But in Genesis 3:1-6 (NIV), you will see how the enemy was able to carry out his plan of deception through the lust of the flesh, the lust of the eyes, and the pride of life:

"Now the serpent was more crafty than any of the wild animals the Lord God had made. He said to the woman [Eve], "Did God really say, 'You must not eat from any tree in the garden'?" The

woman said to the serpent, "We may eat fruit from the trees in the garden, but God did say, 'You must not eat fruit from the tree that is in the middle of the garden, and you must not touch it, or you will die.'" "You will not certainly die," the serpent said to the woman. "For God knows that when you eat from it your eyes will be opened, and you will be like God, knowing good and evil." When the woman saw that the fruit of the tree was good for food [lust of the flesh] and pleasing to the eye [lust of the eye], and also desirable for gaining wisdom [the pride of life], she took some and ate it. She also gave some to her husband [Adam], who was with her, and he ate it."

Because of this, not only did Adam and Eve relinquish the dominion God gave them (Genesis 1:26-28) over to Satan, it also caused sin to enter into the world. This is why God sent Jesus to the earth to be the sacrifice that we needed to restore us back to Himself.

Fear

In most cases, an initial response to fear is to avoid it altogether. This is because of the seriousness that we think this fear carries. However, avoiding fear is how it is able to increase even more. We have a tendency to feel good because we think avoiding the fear is actually working. We may think in our minds that the issue of our fear has been resolved by avoiding it. However, we're deceiving ourselves into believing that it's better to avoid our fears than to face them head-on. As a result, we've just released ourselves over to the same fear we're avoiding and it now has us in bondage.

How Do You Resist the Bait of Fear?

Address your fears with the help of God's strength. When it comes to resisting the bait of fear, one of the first things you must do is acknowledge that you need strength from God in order to defeat fear. When you call on God for His strength, He will then be able to reveal to you what is causing you to have fear with this issue, person, or situation. This can take place in baby steps or it can be done in large leaps, but however you choose to conquer these fears, do it until you are no longer afraid of what is trying to hold you hostage.

Create a list of your fears. As pointless as this may sound, you have no idea how much power this method holds. Just see this as any checklist you make. You will not stop until you have completed or taken care of everything you've written down. Making a list of the fears you have works the same way because the more you see your fears written down (put them in a location where you're able to see them every day), the more you will want to take action against them.

Start by prioritizing your fears from the smallest to the biggest, and let the power of the Lord flow through you from there. Do this one by one until you've revealed and conquered every fear on your list. Reflect on what you've gained and accomplished from the current fear you defeated, and destroy the next fear that is on your list.

Change your thinking. If you want to win the battle against your fears, you have to change the way you are thinking about them. What you are thinking to yourself when you are attacked by fear will determine the outcome of your encounter with it. Are you allowing your thoughts to be connected to God's Word, or are your thoughts taking you in an opposite direction? Come against those thoughts that do not back up what the Father says about fear.

Praise your way through fear. It is necessary to praise your way through fear because praise will lead you into the presence of the Father. When you are focused on giving God praise, fear will not be able to impose. Also from a spiritual realm perspective, praise angers demonic spirits because the last thing they want to hear is you praising God when you should be crying out in fear. Make a daily routine of praising God and as you do, it will cancel out the enemy's plans to send his demonic spirits to you as a way to invoke fear (and keep fear) on you.

Choose to meditate on God's Word, not on your fears. Make a serious effort to meditate on God's Word often, especially the Scriptures that specifically deal with fear. Turn the Scriptures you are reading into daily declarations and affirmations so that you will believe that there is help in meditating on God's Word.

Pray. Prayer is a sure way of connecting to God so that you will be able to destroy your fears. It is a powerful weapon that can be used to set you free from the spirit of fear that has been holding you captive for so long. Allow yourself to connect to prayer to release you so that you can receive the blessings that God has for you.

How Do You Take the Bait of Low Self-Esteem?

There has come a point in all of our lives when we've felt weak, helpless, and condemned. A lot of people are not able to enjoy themselves in life because of the guilt and hopelessness they feel. These are the dangerous and harmful effects of low self-esteem. No Christian should feel that their only choice is to live in a weak and defeated state because the Father saved us from our sins through the sacrifice of His Son Jesus. It's a common reaction for us to feel convicted about things that we do, but it's not normal for us to remain in guilt. Here are a few ways the enemy tries to get us to take the bait of low self-esteem:

Being Accused by Satan

Throughout the Bible, the enemy always found ways to accuse the people of God. He is even described as being the "accuser of the brethren" according to Revelation 12:10. The feeling that comes after the enemy accuses us is condemnation, which if not taken care of immediately, could cause you to become helpless. And this is where you choose to stay because in your mind, there isn't anything that can be done. This isn't the same as conviction that comes from the Holy Spirit when we have sinned. Conviction from the Holy Spirit is needed in order for us to repent and turn from our sins.

Being Hit with Hurtful Words

Some people have a tendency to judge or be too hard on themselves because of the things that were said to them in the past that still sticks with them today. These hurtful words could have come from anybody: friends, parents, guardians, relatives, classmates, teachers, etc. But the reality is, they are still carrying the weight of those words that they heard years ago, causing a bad situation to become worse.

Having the Wrong Attitude About God

If you grew up in an environment where you were pointed out, chastised, and shunned for just about, if not, everything more than you was for the things you did right, this may cause a problem with how you see God. You may feel that you literally have to do everything by God's Book in order to be a Christian so you try to do everything perfect, and when you fail, you probably feel that God is this harsh Being who is waiting to punish you because you missed the mark. This will cause your attitude towards God to take a downward spiral.

Being Reminded of Past Failures

If you constantly reflect on the things that you've failed at in the past, you may begin to feel that you'll never be able to not only move on from that. You may also feel that you will never be able to succeed at anything else. There are sins we may have committed that we feel are so horrible and we hold on to them; the burden of holding on to these sins will terrorize us. We could have chances to enjoy happiness or achieve higher goals, but the thought quickly changes when we think about our past and allow ourselves to feel disappointed and depressed.

Ways to Resist the Bait of Low Self-Esteem

Below are a few ways you can stop the bait of low self-esteem from infiltrating your life:

Stop Believing What Satan Says About You

In John 8:44, Satan is described as being the "father of lies." He has been using lies as far back as the Garden of Eden to cause damage, ruin people's lives, and cause separation between people and God. When the enemy lies about us, he does it in an attempt to damage us so that he feels that he has power over us; when this happens, be mindful of the former part of John 10:10 (ESV) which says, *"The thief comes only to steal and kill and destroy."*

It's time that we become aware of the lies the enemy is trying to use to keep us trapped. During those moments when you find yourself carrying a hopeless mindset, it's the enemy trying to condemn you and that's a problem. But when we are convicted by the Holy Spirit because of our sins, it's only because God wants to give us answers as to how to handle that sin. Conviction comes so that the Holy Spirit can guide us in the right direction, but condemnation comes when the enemy tries to stop us from heading in the right direction.

Start Believing in God's Truth

The Father allowed His Son Jesus to die on the cross so that He could be sacrificed for our sins. Only Jesus was able to pay for a debt He wasn't responsible for. He was completely blameless and even though He knew we all were guilty, He chose to bear our sins anyway. Because of this truth, you can repent for the sins you have committed and know for certain in your heart that your sins have been forgiven. Regardless of how unworthy you felt when you got saved, we all have been covered by the Father's covenant and the blood of Jesus Christ.

Know that You Are Important to God

It's important to know that you are loved by God as you are. You don't have to come to God already "cleaned up" and having it altogether before you decide to give your life to Him. Neither is there a pre-made checklist you must have attached to you to abide by so that God will love you more. The Father loves you just as you are and if you were the only person on this earth, He would still love you. We are a part of God's creation, and we were created to love Him and have a close relationship with Him.

Know that It's OK to Fall Short

We have to come to the realization that Jesus was the only One who was without sin. I don't care how much of a perfectionist you try to be, Christ is the only One who is perfect. There are times when either we have fallen, we're still down from falling, or we're about to fall again but because of God's grace and mercy, we're able to get up. When it comes to the weaknesses that we have, we'll never be able to conquer them on our own. It's only through the strength of God that we'll be able to succeed at gaining the victory over them.

Be Loving and Forgiving when Dealing with Being Accused or Corrected

We all have or will come across someone who will speak words that will cause us to succumb to feelings of being condemned or ashamed if we're not rooted in God. They could be doing this to advise us out of love, or they could be spitefully doing it to try to hurt us. Regardless of the reason, you'll never go wrong if you respond in a manner that is right. Remaining Christ-like is what it's all about; as we continue to respond to accusations and corrections this way, the enemy will be unable to gain a foothold in our lives.

Let Go of Your Past

When you have repented of the sins you have committed, you no longer have to feel weighed down by those sins because whom the Son (Jesus) sets free, is free indeed (John 8:36). Because God has released us from our sins, there's no reason for us to hold on to them any longer; give yourself permission to be set free.

An Example of Not Resisting the Bait of Low Self-Esteem

I had a former friend that I will refer to as "Lisa." She is someone who was a strong, independent Christian woman whom I looked up to. But one of the things I noticed was that most of the topics she would talk about would be pertaining to her past relationships and the issues that were directly and indirectly going on with these men. It just seemed like as time progressed, men, dating, and relationships would be her primary topic and God would be her secondary topic (although she regularly went to church and participated in the activities).

Lisa wasn't old but I guess in her mind, she was. So, the higher she was getting up in age, the more she started saying out loud, "I'm such and such years old; I thought I would've been married by now. I thought I would've had children by now." She would say things like this often as she continued to talk about her past relationships or how she would go out on dates only to be disappointed with men later on down the road. There were times I would tell Lisa, "Enjoy your season of singleness. You're a woman of God, so enjoy your season of singleness. Work for God and He'll bring him (future husband) to you," but it was like it went in one ear and out the other.

Then one day, a man whom I will call "David" who worked with Lisa asked her out on a date. Prior to her going out with David, she would post on social media daily, giving words of encouragement and/or sharing something that was pertaining to God. There were people thanking her for the messages she posted because they were helpful and encouraging. Lisa went out on one date with David and vanished from the social media site she normally posted on. She eventually discontinued her social media account. It was then that I felt, without having met David, that he was the wrong man for her. Because if he was truly sent by God, he would not have blocked her work with God; he would have helped her and enhanced her ministry.

So instead of David being sent by God, he was sent by the enemy as a form of distraction to Lisa. The things she was telling me about David further proved what I was suspecting all along. Without her having to come out and say it, I knew that David was controlling along with other things that caused alarms to go off inside of me. However, Lisa was so desperate to get into a relationship to get out of the current situation she was in at that particular moment, she married this man.

Lisa and I are no longer friends because she allowed David to come between us. In my personal opinion, Lisa was showing David a lot of attention that he wasn't used to getting. He wanted to keep her to himself and consume all of her time, even if that meant keeping her away from those who were originally close to her and a part of her life, including her own family.

Whenever you allow the enemy to convince you that you're getting too old to get married, you thought you would've been married by now, or any other scenario that would cause you to become discouraged, you'll start to lose hope, trust, and faith in God, take the bait of the enemy, and start taking matters into your own hands. That's what Lisa did and as a result, she ended up compromising. There's no telling who God had set aside for Lisa, and we'll never know because of the man she's married to now. She also lost me as a friend in the process because we were growing and gleaning from each other, and the enemy noticed that. He saw that we were close and had a sister-like bond, and he separated us. She realizes that now and doesn't know how to come back around, but I just see it as a closed door and a fact that our friendship was only for a season.

Lisa could've resisted the bait of low self-esteem if she wasn't desperate, but the enemy used David to hook and reel Lisa in. Had she been in a spiritually mature place, she would not have allowed anyone (no matter who they were) to pull her away from God and what she could have been doing for Him today.

How long are you willing to wait in faith for what God has promised you? Will you continue to trust in the Father no matter what you see, or will you allow what you see or have to go through get the best of you? God's timing is not our timing. He knows exactly what to start, stop, pause, and/or change in our lives in order to strengthen our faith so that His promises can be fulfilled for us and through us.

Jesus has conquered death so that we can experience a life of freedom and abundance in Him. The bait that the enemy has set up for us may appear attractive, but the hook of deception he uses to reel us in has serious consequences because it was created to destroy us. Do not allow yourself to live a life that's not on one accord with the life that the Father has for you. Despite the situations you may find yourself in, Jesus can still set you free.

1. B. (2017, September 06). Three Temptations of Sin: Lust of the Flesh, Lust of the Eyes, and the Pride of Life. Retrieved January 23, 2018, from http://www.revelation.co/2015/07/28/three-temptations-of-sin-lust-of-the-flesh-lust-of-the-eyes-and-the-pride-of-life/

11

GROWING MORE IN YOUR
CONFIDENCE

*"The fruit of that righteousness will be peace; its effect will be
quietness and confidence forever."*

— ISAIAH 32:17 (NIV)

What is Confidence?

Confidence is defined as the feeling or belief that one
can rely on someone or something (firm trust). It is
the state of feeling certain about the truth of something or
feeling self-assurance arising from one's appreciation of
one's own abilities or qualities. Confidence is also the telling
of private matters or secrets with mutual trust, or a secret or
private matter told to someone under a condition of trust[1]

From a Christian perspective, confidence is a combination of
what pertains to the characteristics of faith in God, the belief
and guaranteed of a person's commitment to God, a level of

courage that relies on the reality of a person accepting God, and an assurance that a person's future is protected by God.[2]

Was there ever a time when you felt you were lacking in one or all areas of your life? Were you ever assigned a task or placed into a position that was overwhelming to you? I've been there too, but you know what? I appreciate these moments because whenever the Father allows me to be placed in these situations where I feel as if I don't "measure up," I give Him the glory for having confidence in me to be a conqueror.

Having confidence is needed, especially when you are doing the work and the will of God. There are some who may believe that being confident could result in you being conceited and to a certain extent, this is true. However, this is why adding humility to confidence is important.

The more you lack confidence, the more susceptible you become to believing the lies of the enemy. This happens when he tells us that we are not worthy of the Father's love, when he tells us that we lack talent, when he brings our sins back to our remembrance, or convinces us to believe that we will never be good enough for God. But when you are confident with yourself, you will be able to combat these lies so that the Father can do and achieve a great work in us.

The confidence that we have is not based on our gifts, talents, knowledge, or experience; our confidence is what we receive from Jesus. This is what separates confidence from arrogance. When it comes to God, being prideful is the worse trait a Christian could have. The confidence we have should be pure and honest, not mixed with pride. Pride exalts people, but genuine confidence exalts Jesus; this is how He is able to move through us.

When the enemy tries to invoke fear on me or tell me that I don't have what it takes to do God's work, I find myself quickly saying, "*No weapon that is formed against me will ever be able to prosper. I am more than a conqueror through Jesus Christ and what God has called me to do, I will complete.*" This should be the foundation of our confidence and because of that, we have to stop the enemy from trying to take our confidence away from us or trying to stop God's power from moving through us.

Why Is Confidence Important to God?

Confidence allows us to put our full dependence on God in all areas of our lives. We can move along the path He has called us to be on because He is our Leader and Supreme Ruler. When we put our trust in the Father and not in ourselves or other people, it is at this point that we realize we have the Spirit of the living God and Creator of the universe dwelling in us. Isn't that amazing? We can move throughout our lives in a consecrated Christian manner and respond to everything we have to face knowing that all the confidence we need is found in Jesus. Confidence is also when we know that we are responsible for obeying and being faithful to God, but He is responsible for the results of our faith and obedience.

Moving through this life in hesitation, doubt, and lack of trust are some of the opposite characteristics of confidence. Allowing ourselves to conform to this way of thinking will cause us to make decisions out of our restricted view, respond and react out of emotions, and focus on things longer than we should. A lack of confidence will place us in positions to put our trust in ourselves instead of God and hold on to fear because we are focused on our circumstances instead of God.

Confidence should never be centered around wrong reasons. It should never be based on our jobs, titles, positions, social statuses, friends, possessions, achievements, or talents. All of these things that we think are essential for us to make it in life are nothing compared to the wisdom, knowledge, and understanding that we gain from the Father Himself. He doesn't measure our worth based on where we fall on the economic or social scale in society; our worth is based on who we are in Him and the growth and maturity He sees within us. Do not mistake what I'm saying. We should have a desire to be smart and attentive to the decisions we make and make the best of the chances, connections, gifts, and talents we have been allowed to be blessed with. However, the focal point of the choices we make should revolve around Jesus Christ, our Savior. By doing this, we will be able to see that the confidence we have is completely related to where we see ourselves in Him. This should be our form of encouragement in all areas of our lives from the choices we make to the people we connect with and the goals that we have.

God would never tell us to do anything that is not of Him. The assignments He gives us can be seen as an act of Him building up our confidence, and we have to learn to trust Him. For some, this can be hard to do because whenever you try to do things in your own strength instead of relying on God's strength, not only does it show that you lack trust in

God but it's also a sure way to quickly burn yourself out. This could reach the point of you being so exhausted that you end up walking away from the assignment that God has given you so what He wanted to do through you may never be achieved. When the Father calls us to our assignment, He is calling us to His presence; or better yet, His anointing.

How Do You Grow in Your Confidence?

Throughout this book, I have been repeating 2 Timothy 1:7 (KJV) which says, *"For God hath not given us the spirit of fear; but of power, and of love, and of a sound mind."* So, if we are aware of the fact that the spirit of power, love, and a sound mind comes from God, why do we have such a hard time walking in our confidence? The answer is easy: we allow fear to override our confidence. Some people are hesitant about walking in their confidence because fear has taken over them to the point that they think they are going to get rejected or abandoned by others. So many chances are missed when we allow this to happen with the possible result of making a difference for the better in someone's life. So how are you able to move in faith while growing in your confidence?

Allow your confidence to develop in the Holy Spirit. Having the Holy Spirit within us is how the Father is able to strengthen, equip, and prepare us to perform the work that He has for us to do. When Jesus ascended back to heaven, He left the Holy Spirit with us, not the spirits of fear, doubt, worry, or depression. God is aware of the nature of our character, but He is also knows who He is to us and what He has placed inside of us. It is a constant battle to deny your flesh so that you can operate in the Spirit but every time you do, you will increase more in your confidence.

Allow your confidence to develop in your individuality. In 1 Peter 2:9 (ASV), Apostle Peter says:

> *"But ye are an elect race, a royal priesthood, a holy nation, a people for God's own possession, that ye may show forth the excellencies of him who called you out of darkness into his marvelous light."*

We were consecrated by God to carry out His purpose. Because of this, not only will we have traits and gifts, we will also have different appearances and characteristics. The Father has us so tailor-made that He will use what He put in us to stand out to the point that He will allow our paths to cross with others who share the same distinctions we have. No matter how "different" you think you are, God can still use you for the glory of His Kingdom. Just because you are an ambassador for Christ doesn't mean you have to become someone you're not in order to be used by God. Have confidence in being the person the Father has shaped and molded you to be for Him. In doing this, you will become clothed in the nature of Jesus with a desire to be more like Him so that you can be used by Him in order to touch the lives of others.

Allow your confidence to develop in Jesus. When we know who we are in Jesus, we can have more assurance about how He sees us through His eyes. No matter what we think or how we feel about ourselves, God can still use us for His benefit. As you choose to receive His acceptance of you, your confidence will become more established in who you are.

You will be able to happily walk as the person God has created you to be and embrace what makes you stand out. You will look forward to the opportunities to strengthen your confidence while you are submitting yourself more to the Father and allowing yourself to be a willing vessel for Him.

See yourself as God sees you. God has an assignment for each of us, but each of them are special and specifically created for each of us. Regardless of how you try to measure yourself, the Father still believes that He can use you. You may feel that you're just an ordinary person and there's nothing special about you, but you felt led to pick up your phone and call a friend not knowing at that particular moment that they just got hit with some bad news. Or God used you to help someone who was having a difficult time, or give money and/or food to the person who's standing out on the street holding up a sign. However God chooses to use us, He will do it so that we can be the light to others when He needs us to be. So, what you think about your "shortcomings" is irrelevant. What you may find as being incomplete within yourself is just what the Father wants to use to complete His work through you; the more you receive this and act on it, the more your confidence will remain anchored in God.

Where Do You Begin with Christian (Bible-Based) Affirmations?

Begin by writing down every negative word, criticism, or judgment you or others have said or felt about you. If it came from someone else, do not dwell on it; that way, you can avoid bitterness and unforgiveness to form about them. After you do this, begin to write down your affirmations by turning the negative words into positive statements that are connected to God and/or His Word. For example, if someone called you ugly, write down a positive affirmation that says, "I am fearfully and wonderfully made" (Psalm 139:14). Instead of saying to yourself, "I don't have this" or "I need that," write down an affirmation that says, "God, my Father, will supply all of my need according to His riches in glory in Christ Jesus" (Philippians 4:19).

Christian affirmations can also establish where you would like to be or what you would like to accomplish in life. For example, a positive affirmation you can say about having success would be, "God's Word will not leave my mouth because I will meditate on it day and night and do what is written in it and by doing this, my ways will become prosperous, and I will have good success (Joshua 1:8)." Try to speak these affirmations a few minutes at a time throughout the day; reflect and meditate on what you are saying and believe that what you are saying is true. If need be, write your affirmations down on paper, or in a journal, because the more you write them down, the more you will be to remember them. So, if circumstances try to revisit you, you can combat and destroy those negative seeds with the Father's positive Word of encouragement.

---

1. (n.d.). Retrieved January 23, 2018, from https://www.google.com/search?q=Dictionary#dobs=confidence
2. Confidence Definition and Meaning - Bible Dictionary. (n.d.). Retrieved January 23, 2018, from https://www.biblestudytools.com/dictionary/confidence/

CONCLUSION

Congratulations for making it to the end of this book - I'm so proud of you! I know that this was a lot for you to digest but by reflecting and applying everything you've read, you are now more than prepared to face your fears head-on so that you can embrace the confidence that God has for you to receive. This is only the beginning for you; it gets better from here! What this book comes down to is this: the more you feed your confidence, the less room fear will have to operate in your life.

When it comes to fear and confidence, both sides of the spectrum are before you but the side you choose to accept or ignore will be the side that either strengthens or weakens you. The Father wants you to walk confidently in the life He has given you. He doesn't want you to live your life in fear because it will delay you, cause you to live in bondage, or stop your progression altogether. This is not the way God intended for you to live. Choose to live in the confidence and freedom that He has tailored and custom-fit just for you!

CALL TO ACTION

Although you have made it to the end of this book, you may still be asking yourself, "Where do I go now? What happens from here?" Well, one of the things I recommend you do is read this book again and process what you are reading because I assure you that the more you read this book, the more insight you will receive the next time around. You will be able to read this in a new way and equip yourself even more. The second thing I suggest you do is get a copy of this book for someone else. If you know someone who has allowed fear to be a place of comfort for them, purchase this book for them so that they will know that greater is in store for them to receive on the other side of fear.

PRAYERS

Altar Call Prayers
For Those Who Want to Give Their Lives to Christ

"If you confess with your mouth that Jesus is Lord, and believe in your heart that God raised him from the dead, you will be saved."

— ROMANS 10:9 (WEB)

This type of prayer is commonly referred to as the salvation prayer. The prayer of salvation is powerful and because of this, it's your faith in God for His Son Jesus that is going to save you. Please let the following prayer sincerely flow from your heart, and have faith in knowing that you will be new person in Christ after you say it:

Jesus, I am aware of the fact that prior to now, I did not live my life for You. Instead, I have been making my life about me and not including You in it. I now see that I need You in my life, and

I invite You to come into my life. I am a sinner, and I'm sorry for the sins that I have committed against You. I know that God sent You to earth to complete the finished work on the cross at Calvary by allowing Your life to be a sacrifice for my sins, and I thank You for that. I know that You did this for me so that I could be forgiven and set free from all of the sins that I have committed. You offered, and I accept Your gift of salvation. Please turn my stony heart into a heart of flesh on this day. Come into my life and live inside of my heart because I acknowledge and accept You as my Lord and Savior. Wash me clean with Your powerful, anointed blood, and set me free from Satan and the snares and traps of this world that he is trying to keep me entangled in. No more will I choose to walk in sin. Instead, I choose to walk in the ways that are favorable and pleasing to You. I turn my back on the world and choose to take up my cross and follow You this day and each day to come. In Your Name, Jesus, I pray, Amen.

For Those Who Want to Rededicate Their Lives to Christ

"Create in me a clean heart, O God, and renew a right spirit within me."

— PSALM 51:10 (ESV)

"Therefore, I urge you, brothers and sisters, in view of God's mercy, to offer your bodies as a living sacrifice, holy and pleasing to God--this is your true and proper worship. Do not conform to the pattern of this world, but be transformed by the renewing of your mind. Then you will be able to test and approve what God's will is--his good, pleasing and perfect will."

— ROMANS 12:1-2 (NIV)

A rededication prayer expresses a change of heart for God and a desire to return to Him. If you need to rededicate your life back to Christ, please repeat the following prayer:

God, I just want to say thank You for not only hearing me when I pray to You, but for also being patient with me. I am returning to You because I am able to find refuge in You by reading Your Word and accepting the promises you made for me in Your Word. Choosing to make the decision to rededicate my life back to Christ means that I am making the decision to do what is important for my eternal salvation. I am coming back to You because all of the love, acceptance, and forgiveness that I need and have been looking for is found in You.

Jesus, thank You for loving me and accepting me as I am. Thank You for showing me that You are the way, the truth, and the life. You are forgiving and compassionate, and I thank You for that. The grace and mercy You show and have for me is amazing. I repent for turning my back on You, and I repent for all of the sins that I have committed against You - known and unknown. I rededicate my life back to You, and I'm exchanging my will for Your will. I'm moving myself out of the way, and I give You permission to take over my life this day and each day to follow. In Your Name, Jesus, I pray, Amen.

Warfare Prayer to Break the Spirit of Fear

Father, I am coming to You with a confident heart. You told me in Your Word to be strong and not fear because You will come with vengeance and divine retribution; You will come to save me (Isaiah 35:4). It is Your peace you give to me so therefore, I receive Your peace today. Father, I will not let my heart be troubled, nor will I be afraid (John 14:27). At Your command, I choose to be strong and courageous instead of afraid and discouraged because I know You will be with me wherever I go (Joshua 1:9). I will not be afraid because You redeemed me and You have summoned me by my name because I am Yours (Isaiah 43:1).

Even though I walk through the darkest valley, I will not fear evil because You are with me; Your rod and Your staff, they comfort me (Psalm 23:4). I sought You, and You answered me by saying that You delivered me from all of my fears (Psalm 34:4). When anxiety was heavy on me, Your consolation brought me joy (Psalm 94:19). Father, You are My light and salvation - Whom shall I fear? You are the strength of my life - Of whom shall I be afraid (Psalm 27:1)? I will humble myself under Your mighty hand so that in due time, You will lift me up. I will cast all of my anxiety on You because You care for me (1 Peter 5:6-7). Father, I have no reason to be afraid of what anyone does to me because You are with me (Psalm 118:6). You haven't given me the spirit of fear, but of power, love, and a sound mind (2 Timothy 1:7). I believe that You are my help and shield because I fear and trust in You (Psalm 115:11).

I pray that I will continue to be strong and courageous. I will not be afraid or terrified of anyone because You, Father, go with me, and You will never leave me or forsake me (Deuteronomy

31:6). *During those times when I find myself afraid, I pray that I will put my trust in You. I will praise Your Word, Father. I will trust You and not be afraid of anything anyone does to me because I know that You are with me (Psalm 56:3-4). I pray that You will continue to strengthen, help, and uphold me with Your right hand (Isaiah 41:10).*

Father, You told me not to be afraid because I will not be put to shame. May I not fear disgrace because I will not be humiliated (Isaiah 54:4). I pray that I will be on guard, stand firm in the faith, and remain courageous and faithful (1 Corinthians 16:13). May I continue to know, understand, and realize that there is no fear in love because perfect love drives out fear. If I choose to fear, I'm not made perfect in love (1 John 4:18).

Lastly, Father, I thank You for delivering me from the spirit of fear. I give you the glory for binding and casting out every stronghold of the enemy coming against me. I thank You, Father, for giving me the confidence in knowing that You are for me and You are with me. I can walk in confidence because there's nothing I will face today that You are not able to see me through, nor is there anything or anyone else greater than You. May I continue to rest in Your arms because no weapon that is formed against me will ever be able to prosper (Isaiah 54:14). I give You the glory for making me victorious and freely giving me Your salvation and Your peace which surpasses all understanding (Philippians 4:7). In Jesus' Name I pray, Amen.

OTHER WORKS

In 2018, LaShana was featured in an anthology titled *"You Have No Idea the Hell I've Been Through: 22 Women Who Pushed from Pain to Purpose."* In this powerful, bestselling book, LaShana discusses how she witnessed abuse in her home and being sexually abused as a child, as well as her experience with being blackballed from the military. But, with all glory going to God, she was able to forgive, be healed from her past, and allow what she went through to contribute greatly to the purpose the Father has for her. For more information about this book and how to order it, visit www.youhavenoideabooks.com.

ABOUT THE AUTHOR

LaShana Lloyd is a Christian author, blogger, speaker, and life coach for women. She helps women from all walks of life become encouraged, inspired, and empowered so that they can grow stronger in their confidence.

In 2016, LaShana launched Faith Led Life and Faith Led Life Coaching, LLC. She was amazed at how excited women were searching to improve in the different areas of their lives. LaShana's vision is to reach the hearts of women around the world so that they can receive the Glory of Jesus, and teach them the importance of establishing a relationship with God through the Holy Spirit with encouragement and inspiration. Her mission is to prepare women by nourishing their souls with spoken or written words that will lead them to or back to God with a passion-driven purpose to inspire and support women to walk in their calling, and equip them to receive the Father's glory.

LaShana is being led by faith to do the things that must be done for God's glory. It is her prayer that her ministry will lead other women back to God with the words that she writes and speaks. It is also LaShana's desire that women will find encouragement in her because of her walk with God, which will prepare them to receive more of God or receive Him for the first time. LaShana strongly believes that women of faith will come from her ministry, and she will prepare them to do greater work for God's Kingdom.

Christian Life Coaching for Women

As a life coach, LaShana serves women who have gone through painful, traumatic experiences by using inner healing techniques to help them regain their wholeness. She inspires her clients to seek the Lord's will and align their lives with God's plan. LaShana helps her clients reach certain goals and/or gives encouragement to them when they are facing changes or transitions in their lives. She also uses coaching knowledge and tools to assist her clients in finding their talents and gifts to benefit a greater purpose, and she uses prayer to assist in the removal of obstacles presented by the enemy (Satan).

Confidence-Building Session

You can schedule a free 30-minute Confidence-Building Session with me. During this session, we will work together on creating a clear vision for the kind of life God has intended you to live and uncovering hidden challenges that may be sabotaging your purpose. After your call is complete, you will leave the session renewed, encouraged, and inspired to walk in the faith and confidence that God has given to you.

You can schedule a Confidence-Building Session with me by going to www.faithledlife.com. You will then go to my Coaching Page and click on the link. You will be taken to a form that you will have to fill out so that I can get to know who you are and how we can get you moving forward in your confidence. From there, you will be taken to my calendar page where you can select a day and time that you prefer to schedule your call with me.

Contact Information

Website: www.faithledlife.com

Email: info@faithledlife.com

Facebook: faithledlifeofficial

LinkedIn: faithledlife

Pinterest: @faithledlife

Twitter: @FaithLedLife

Instagram: @faithledlifeofficial

Clubhouse: @faithledlife